UNFUCK YOUR NONPROFIT

Dr. Faith G. Harper, ACS, ACN
and Joe Biel

UNFUCK YOUR NONPROFIT

Change the World Without Losing Your Mind or Values

Dr. Faith G. Harper, ACS, ACN
and Joe Biel

Microcosm Publishing

Portland, Oregon | Cleveland, Ohio

UNFUCK YOUR NONPROFIT: *Change the World Without Losing Your Mind or Values*

© Dr. Faith G. Harper and Joe Biel, 2026

First edition - 3,000 copies - February 3, 2026
ISBN 9781648414879
This is Microcosm # 837
Edited by Katie Haegele
Cover illustration by Gerta Oparaku
Cover and design by Joe Biel and Sarah Koch

This edition © Microcosm Publishing, 2026
For a catalog, write or visit:
Microcosm Publishing
2752 N Williams Ave.
Portland, OR 97227

All the news from the misfits in print at Microcosm.Pub/Newsletter
Get more copies of this book at Microcosm.pub/UnfuckYourNonprofit

EU Safety Information: microcosmpublishing.com/gpsr

Library of Congress Control Number: 2025043403

In the U.S. COMO (Atlantic), ABRAHAM (Midwest), BOB BARNETT (Texas, Arkansas, Oklahoma, Louisiana), IMPRINT (Pacific), TURNAROUND (Europe), UTP/MANDA (Canada), NEWSOUTH (Australia/New Zealand), Observatoire (Africa, Europe), IPR (Middle East), Yvonne Chau (Southeast Asia), HarperCollins (India), Everest/B.K. Agency (China), Tim Burland (Japan/Korea), or FAIRE in the gift trade.Did you know that you can buy our books directly from us at sliding scale rates? Support a small, independent publisher and pay less than Amazon's price at www.Microcosm.Pub.

Global labor conditions are bad, and our roots in industrial Cleveland in the '70s and '80s made us appreciate the need to treat workers right. Therefore, our books are MADE IN THE USA.

Microcosm's workers and authors are paid solely from book sales. If you downloaded this book from some sketchy part of the Internet or picked up what appears to be a bootleg, please support our hardworking team by purchasing a copy directly from us and encouraging your communities to do the same. Paying for our books and zines helps us publish work that's far better than anything AI can come up with. Additionally, a 2025 MIT study revealed that AI inhibits humanity's critical thinking ability. Since critical thinking is one of our core values, we prohibit any use of our books to "train" generative artificial "intelligence" (AI) technologies, because seriously, WTF?

MICROCOSM·PUBLISHING

Microcosm Publishing is Portland's most diversified publishing house and distributor, with a focus on the colorful, authentic, and empowering. Our books and zines have put your power in your hands since 1996, equipping readers to make positive changes in their lives and in the world around them. Microcosm emphasizes skill-building, showing hidden histories, and fostering creativity through challenging conventional publishing wisdom with books and bookettes about DIY skills, food, bicycling, gender, self-care, and social justice. What was once a distro and record label started by Joe Biel in a drafty bedroom was determined to be *Publishers Weekly*'s fastest-growing publisher of 2022 and #3 in 2023 and 2024, and is now among the oldest independent publishing houses in Portland, OR, and Cleveland, OH. We are a politically moderate, centrist publisher in a world that has inched to the right for the past 80 years.

C⚙NTENTS

INTRODUCTION

What actually is a nonprofit? Is it necessarily good?

A nonprofit is a business.

Now, stay with us: you know we're not wrong.

Every nonprofit is a business . . . but it is one that purportedly has a mission/priority beyond making money. Confusingly, a nonprofit *can* make a profit. Any revenue brought in is (usually) folded back into the program to keep the organization operating. The nonprofit dimension of the organization is often a form of marketing and branding that attempts to proclaim, "We aren't like those other corporations!"

Additionally, the organization is exempt from paying taxes as an institutional reward for providing a community benefit. Tax exemptions are just for the organization itself; the employees who work there still pay income tax.[1] Tax exemption means there is extra paperwork and reports and audits at certain levels that need to be attended to in order to maintain this tax-exempt status, but it allows the organization to be free from a heavy tax bill, and also allows it to apply for pools of "free" money (grants from government organizations, private foundations, individual sponsors, and donors) to utilize in support of their stated mission, because again, "We aren't like *those* corporations."

Business-minded outlets like the *Harvard Business Review* have published honest but frustrating articles about how the nonprofit market and the for-profit market are so similar, it may make more

1 And to get even more granular, if you are curious? A nonprofit still pays payroll taxes, which are split between the employee and the agency (FICA, Social Security, Medicare). *Except.* Nonprofits are exempt from having to pay the Federal Unemployment Tax Act (FUTA) tax, which provides unemployment benefits. FUTA is the one federal tax that only the company is responsible for paying.

sense for a start-up to get funded if they organize themselves as a nonprofit. And an article in *Forbes* suggested that entrepreneurs at least start a not-for-profit arm of any business because it builds goodwill and lends trustworthiness to their enterprise. Which is also an honest-but-wtf take on being a successful business. Whether you lean all in or partially in, the word is out: a 501(c)(3) is a useful tool.

Which upsets our little cruster-punk, do-gooder souls. We wrote this book because we want to reframe the conversation about nonprofits and focus on their primary value proposition, which is allegedly to *help people*, and talk about how to get them back to that focus.

Where did nonprofits come from?

The term 501(c)(3) comes from the Internal Revenue Service (IRS) and is the main category that nonprofits fall in. Other terms you may see are: 527 [a political operation], 501(c)(4) [a social welfare organization], $501(c)(6)^2$ [a business league], and $501(c)(7)$ [social and recreation clubs]. The numbers in these designations come from the federal laws that set the standard for organizations that are generally exempt from federal income taxes.

You may also see the initialisms NP (nonprofit), NFP (not-for-profit), NPO (nonprofit organization), and NFPO (not-for-profit organization). And you will see us use them all throughout this book so you can get used to the associated cultural lingo, because we are supportive like that.

NPOs are not just a business, they are *big* business. The US Bureau of Labor Statistics tracks such data in the US, and they note that the NPO sector of the whole ouroboros of the American

---

2 You know who was a $501(c)(6)$ nonprofit until 2015? The NFL. The NFL was founded in 1920, and it became an NFP in 1942. Congress passed the Sports Broadcasting Act in 1961, giving the NFL an antitrust exemption, while maintaining a tax-exempt status as long as they allowed games to be broadcast nationally. The NFL, in return, saved ten million dollars a year in taxes. They gave it up in 2015 once people became aware of their bullshit (and the fact that they were blacking out games in various locales all along). So yes, a nonprofit is absolutely a business.

economy (and our gross domestic product) is one of the largest, making up more than a tenth of the American workforce (only beaten out by manufacturing and retail). They report that in 2022, over 300,000 nonprofits provided 12.8 million jobs. NFPs existed in all sectors of industry, but unsurprisingly healthcare and social assistance account for two-thirds of these jobs. The highest rate of nonprofit employment? Washington, DC, where one out of every four employed individuals works for a nonprofit.[3]

And that 12.8 million jobs (within 300,000 agencies) is based on such a small percentage of non-profits operating in the U.S. Keep in mind that about 1.8 million agencies are registered with the IRS, and wider estimates show that there are likely about 2.5 million organizations total, as smaller grassroots organizations and congregations are not required to formally register.

---

3 DC isn't at all surprising as a choice. Lobbyists, BAYBEEE.

Where does all this money go?

Okay, now the money. How much of it is flowing through all of these agencies? Amanda Montell, one of the hosts of the podcast *Sounds Like A Cult*, pointed out the following on their "Cult of Nonprofits" episode:

> *The Salvation Army made $2.37 billion in private donations and a $4.1 billion total revenue in 2021. Feeding America—$3.4 billion in private, $3.5 billion in total revenue. St. Jude's was like $2 billion in private donations. United Way worldwide made $3.85 billion in private donations and $5.2 billion in total revenue.* **Why are there still hungry people?**

These are four of the largest NPOs in the US, and all of them work with food insecurity. So why hasn't over $10B per year eliminated food insecurity?

Overall, the amount of money that flows through these programs is breathtaking. Statistics compiled by Donorbox, an online fundraising platform, demonstrate that the amount of money flowing through these organizations has gone up between 2000 and 2024 (the time of their report). Donorbox states that the total revenue of nonprofits has grown from just over $1 trillion in 2000 to about $3T. The National Council on Nonprofits notes that the total expenses of all of these organizations in 2022 was $2.46T.

So. American nonprofits are spending trillions and taking in even more (remember, you are still allowed to make a profit for some fucking reason). GlobalGiving, a nonprofit that connects nonprofits to donors, estimates that the cost of ending hunger *worldwide* is between $7-265 billion per year. That's 11% of the money flowing through US-based organizations alone. Why are there still hungry people, indeed? Where is the money going if it's not ending world hunger? Are nonprofits inefficient at their goals, or are they dishonest?

Why are *no* social problems actually fixed? Why are none of these organizations saying

"Mission accomplished! Now we close up shop!"? One major reason is that, as Amanda Montell said on the podcast *Sounds Like A Cult,* "nonprofits are not incentivized to solve the problems that they set out to, because then they wouldn't exist anymore . . . this is accepted because the nonprofit label is deified." Like all other businesses, they are incentivized to stay in funding cycles and compete with other agencies for funding—often reshaping their mission to match funder and donor goals, as many agency leaders reported to the Urban Institute when asked about their top concerns going into 2025. Competition instead of inter-agency collaboration . . . while shifting the focus of the work in order to seem more appealing to those who write the checks.

Some of the 990 data from Feeding America demonstrate this disconnect without having to do a deep dive into all their filing and their annual reports. For example, Feeding America, like the American Red Cross, is designated as a four-star charity by Charity Navigator. It's fully considered one of the good guys. And y'all? They have *bank*. The 2023 filings (the most recent at the time of this writing) demonstrate that their revenue was $5.05 billion. That is a motherfucking "B."

Some of their more local offshoots that also pop up have revenue in the millions. Furthermore, the Feeding America executive team are bringing home nice paychecks. Their CEO, Claire Babineaux Fontenot, brought home $949,866 in salary and $163,636 in other compensation in 2023. And they have a plethora of people in the C-suite and at the VP level making a quarter of a million to half a million in that same filing year.

And hey, they're well-funded, so why not compensate adequately? We mean, sure. But are people getting fed? By an agency whose only job is announced in the title of the agency? Our podcaster bestie, Amanda Montell, asked why there are so many hungry people. And apparently, Feeding America is also confused by the question and decided they needed to do research into that as well. Their Statement of Program Service

Accomplishments in their tax filings included a nugget about their Research and Evaluation team needing to do *"critical research initiatives to better understand hunger."*

What did that cost in 2023? They spent $85M in order to, in their words, *"better understand hunger and to continually improve our strategies to end it. We analyze the dynamics at play among the Nation's food insecure individuals and families, the patterns surrounding their use of our services, and endeavor to utilize this data to ultimately create better local feeding programs."* That is to say, they spent $85M in **just one year** to study the dynamic of hungry people, instead of simply feeding them.

The statement goes on about how their research arm is focused on bullshit—sorry, we mean *concerns*, about timely neighbor insights (what does this mean?) and racial inequalities (at least that's a phrase that makes sense!). Go read it if you dig, it's a bop.

But. But. *But.*

The part we want to point out, in big, backlit, neon letters is how much this "research" cost. Just in that one year's tax return they spent $85,401,590 on this "vital" research and development. Eighty-five million motherfucking dollars? That didn't go to feeding *people*? Hey Amanda? Holler at us if you ever want to revisit that episode with an update, because we found one big reason that there are still so many hungry people. Eighty-five million motherfucking dollars would feed about *30,000 families for a year*. For many agencies like this, they cannot relate with the people that they serve, so they get lost in the weeds of how to serve them. This disconnect worsens when they wield eight-figure budgets and don't focus them on the single goal of the organization. And that's the disconnect that we aim to address in this book.

Who are we?

Now let's get back to why we came here. Your authors, Joe and Faith, both have extensive histories with the NPO market.

Faith has been both a not-for-profit worker and, later in her career, a fancy-pantsy board member of more than one program. Her experiences lean hard into mental health and human rights, which is no surprise to anyone. She also is a constant supporter of other mechanisms of community care, like mutual aid organizations. As of press time, Joe serves on two boards and advises on a third—after proposing and leading a fourth through an asset acquisition in 2024! (An "asset acquisition" is a fancy way of saying that the organization merged with another. But combining two nonprofits is much more expensive, so it's usually easier and cheaper for the surviving one to own everything that the surrendering one had.) In addition, Joe has consulted for and witnessed the inner workings of dozens of other nonprofits. While nonprofits are thought of very differently from business, the actual differences are pretty miniscule, and Faith and Joe have both been in business for decades as well.

We have written a dozen other books together. Three of them in particular are likely applicable, as much as you may not see it this way. *Unfuck Your Business* outlines a lot of the particulars of thinking about and running an operation. We don't repeat that stuff here, because frankly, most of the same stuff applies to any organization in terms of output and leverage. The problems that plague nonprofits are the problems that plague businesses. Or—as reviewer Jeremy Markey said of *Unfuck Your Business*, "clear-eyed decision-making, systems thinking, and the importance of overcoming internal obstacles . . . a great book." He honestly makes our book sound really great and summarizes our core principles in it thusly:

- Hope is not a business strategy.

- Don't scale dysfunction.

- Math doesn't lie, but people sure do.

- Unclear expectations are premeditated resentment.

- Clear is kind.

- If everything is a priority, nothing is.

- Entrepreneurship is 10% vision and 90% logistics.

- Boundaries are the blueprint for success.

- Growth is not the same as success.

- If you can't explain your business model in one sentence, you don't have one.

- Respect the math, your feelings don't get a vote.

- Start small and iterate.

- Talk about your problems.

- Set clear boundaries and expectations.

- Know your niche.

- Focus on systems.

- Let go of imposter syndrome.

- Create calming, grounding routines for your brain space to process ideas.

A major reason that we wrote that book is because we were so unhappy with the existing books on the shelf. So perhaps it's no surprise that, when summarized in this way, it sounds really great.

Even if you don't read it, please make sure to follow the advice above.

The *Unfuck Your Business Workbook* expands on these ideas and exercises into specifics for assessing new programs, testing ideas, and measuring how well things are working for you. It also has a lot of exercises about how you may be getting in your own way. Joe created a chart for determining the viability of an idea based on graphing it. Many of the other ideas explored in the workbook are new and independent of the accompanying handbook, since we wrote the workbook a year later.

Similarly, *Managing Neurodiverse Workplaces* is (surprise!) a great, best-practices manual for managing *any* organization. Why? Well, it turns out that neurodiverse people need the same things that everyone else does. Those needs just get expressed in different ways. This book was a product of a very stressful five years during which dozens of employees had various crises. We learned a lot about when to give grace, when to hold a boundary, when people need special accommodations, and when going too far out on a limb for one person is actively harming the rest of your team. Or worse—when doing too much for one person communicates to the rest of your team what the culture of your organization is. It tells them, "when this happens, this is how we handle it." Or sometimes, even worse: "If you do this, this is how it will be discussed within the organization." Sometimes seeing the inner workings of how an employee's crisis is handled causes your best people to hesitate. Other times it lowers the bar. In all cases, you are setting the expectations and motivations for your entire staff as they watch how you manage everyone else.

We think of those three books, plus this one, as a sort of suite for running an organization. This book is the framework for how to think of a nonprofit and apply the more unique principles to its operation. *Unfuck Your Business* has a lot of the nitty-gritty mechanical tools and advice on getting past aspects of your childhood or limited experience in life that is holding you back. The *Workbook* is similar but has more specific exercises to your organization, plans, ideas, and programs. Then, once you have staff, *Managing Neurodiverse Workplaces* is the key to supporting those employees in the way that suits them and their needs. Because ultimately, it's your job to provide everyone with the support each person needs so that you all win. These books were born out of 30 years of experience.

Additionally, some other books to check out include Bernard Kamoroff's *Small Time Operator*—which contains immense lessons from a seasoned accountant on the minutiae of understanding money coming and going, and what the tax man needs to know—and Paul Hawken's classic *Growing a Business.* Hawken founded a company that imported higher-quality British gardening tools to the U.S. and has many good lessons about the strength of exploring your own vision and ideas to the limits of where your constituents will follow you. His best point is that nobody can steal your idea because nobody else could pull it off quite right or they would miss the important detail that you understand fundamentally—because it's your idea.

Why are we qualified to claim that we're experts on nonprofits in particular? Well, we've both been (vastly underpaid) employees and board members who went into these roles wanting to contribute to the world-saving, and later left the roles feeling hopeless, frustrated, and sometimes downright furious. And it got us thinking (and talking) about how to do this work in ways that align with our progressive values and determination to affect real change in our communities.

When a nonprofit says that they "can't afford" something, we look up their public filings, assess waste, and compare their means to our own. They are almost always in a better position to pay for something than we are—and neither of us is close to starving. Presumably, you also have progressive values and a determination to affect real change in your communities. So how can we re-center what we all came to do? How can we start a program from the ground up that's steeped in direct action and community care? Or, how can we go into programs that have lost their way and advocate a move back to these same values? This book is the result of all that questioning. Not just based on what passes our particular vibe check, but also what the data bears out.

(Remember, Faith and Joe are researchers and have done data analytics for numerous nonprofits. We know where the numbers are buried, and we're going to take you on an excavation for them as we present our case.)

This book isn't intended to be an indictment of the industry as it stands, but a tough look at how it stands and how we can *do better*. While making sure you, as a fellow let's-do-better traveler, have the tools you need (including some juicy unearthed data) to give you a shot in hell to make that happen.

So yeah, this is our own version of the ten commandments. But pretty sure we don't say "thou shalt" or "thou shalt not" anywhere on the following pages.[4] So let's get to work.

---

4 A very early outline of this book did include that language. But we are old and our backs hurt too much to be twee, so we fixed that pretty early on.

YOU MIGHT NOT NEED TO BE A NONPROFIT

*W*e all want a better world, right? We may each define that a little differently, but that's something uniting us. And when we are thinking about solving societal struggles, nonprofit organizations are the first entities that most people think of. But there are many ways to participate in making the world a better place, and you can do so without going near the NPO industrial complex. Depending on what your long-term goals are, avoiding NPOs might just work even better.

You can start a for-profit business that still focuses on the exact same social good. When Joe founded Microcosm, the publisher of this book, in 1996, the original vision was to form the organization as a nonprofit. Joe researched the requirements, which are primarily:

- maintaining an overseeing board of directors;

- operating pursuant to a mission statement;

- publicly publishing finances annually;

- reinvesting profits into the organization;

- and quite a bit of initial and ongoing paperwork.

Joe wanted to provide tools to change people's lives and the world around them, while providing a transparent operation so that people could see that we were utilizing every dollar in a smart manner towards distributing these materials globally. Since the requirements for operating a nonprofit are all core tenets of Microcosm, running the organization as an NPO seemed like a great way to show the intention of the project.

However, dozens of people from the Nonprofit Industrial Complex immediately warned and strongly cautioned Joe that this would water down and undermine the ability of the organization to be effective at its mission. Numerous people shared stories of NFPs whose boards fired the founder because they didn't understand performance indicators about the organization's effectiveness, or reduced employee compensation until it would be impossible for anyone to work there. But in most cases, the story behind the story was that once a grassroots project became a nonprofit, the organization became so mired in red tape that it was bureaucratically inefficient or lost sight of goals. A friend with a degree in nonprofit management pleaded, "Every time I have witnessed a functional organization converted into a nonprofit, the results are horrifying."

So instead of going the NFP route, Joe founded Microcosm as a Limited Liability Corporation, filing as a partnership with an employee stock ownership plan that also happens to follow the public accountability responsibilities of a nonprofit, such as publishing finances annually.[5] For many organizations, the reason they form legal entities as nonprofits is to take advantage of the perception, marketing, and branding that nonprofits receive. Simply put, 57% of Americans report high trust in nonprofits in 2025,[6] while 71% of Americans have a negative view of corporations.[7] It's funny because the difference between the two is mostly paperwork and semantics.

Today, Microcosm continues to operate pursuant to the operating rules of a nonprofit,

---

5 Over the past 30 years, numerous people have said that they would have been fine giving artwork or labor for free to Microcosm if it was "a legitimate nonprofit." This speaks to the public misunderstanding that there really is very little distinction between the two, as well as the depth of marketing and branding about the NFP world.

6 "Trust in Nonprofits and Philanthropy," Independent Sector

7 "Anti-corporate sentiment in the U.S. is now widespread in both parties," Amina Dunn and Andy Cerda, Pew Research Center.

except without having a board. While Microcosm *could* have a board of advisors and this is something that we are open to in the future, we don't see any advantages to adding another layer of bureaucracy on top of managers and staff. Like any other legally mandated layer of anything, having a board of directors can be really helpful, with some management, to create great direction— or it can lead the organization on a series of wild goose chases.

All this to say: you can start a for-profit business with a social enterprise mission. Social enterprise businesses combine a market-driven approach with a desire to engender social change. Toms Shoes is an example of a social enterprise business, where whenever a pair of their shoes is purchased, they donate a second pair to someone in need. (There are issues with their model, which we'll discuss later in this book . . . but it was a lovely impulse on the part of founder Blake Mycoskie from the get-go.)

Ben & Jerry's, in its Vermont infancy, was a great example of a social enterprise business. The founders used their success to fund activism that was dear to their hearts. They truly showed themselves in their brand and advertising. Ben and Jerry, the people, created their own foundation and placed 7.5% of their pre-tax profits in a fund for activism. The business was a funnel to express their values, donating over $50M across the past 40 years. They sold the company to Unilever in 2000, and dramatically reduced their donations from being a direct percentage of profits to a variable annual allocation. This severs the direct responsibility of profits to social responsibility spending. In 2025, when the foundation refused to provide details to Unilever about how much money they were providing to Palestinian aid charities, Unilever cut their funding by millions.

Warby Parker, similar to Toms, provides a donated pair of glasses for each one sold. But perhaps—like many online companies who have streamlined a bloated business model—their greatest strength is in dramatically slashing retail prices for glasses. The world is shifting towards businesses that make a positive impact and consumers wanting to support them. In a 2014 poll, 94% of millennials said that they wanted to work for a social enterprise business to "use their skills for good."[8] Simultaneously, consumers are sharply motivated by the idea that they are advocating for their values with their dollars, and this is reinforced in dozens of studies.

Some social enterprise businesses also apply for a public benefit corporation status (B-Corp). B-Corp certifications are a higher standard of social enterprise companies, and they undergo a rigorous process of demonstrating that while they are for-profit, they value social and environmental goals. B-Corps are certified through a global nonprofit network known as B-Lab. Faith, when wanting to purchase a pair of crocheted clogs, bought them through The Sak, which is a B-Corp

---

8 achievecauses.com/wp-content/uploads/2025/05/ MIR_2014-2020.pdf

business that focuses on sustainable practices and pays fair wages and provides healthcare to the artisans who make the clogs in Bali. And they're great; Faith is still wearing the same pair she bought a few years ago on the regular. She's a fan.

And let's remember that "for profit" doesn't mean that there *is* a profit, and at the same time, a "nonprofit" *can* have a profit. The magic is in the finances of each individual organization.

You know what's awesome? Mutual aid.

And hey, maybe you lean more in our direction in that you don't want to start a business, you really just want to help people, full-stop. You can do that through a not-for-profit or a for-profit business, as we've just shown, or you can do that through mutual aid. In an article published by *Vice* early in the COVID-19 pandemic, Lexi McMenamin demarcated the difference between mutual aid and charitable organizations perfectly:

Mutual aid is also not charity: rather than creating a centralized organization where one person is giving to someone else, forcing them to become dependent on yet another relationship negotiating their access to material resources, mutual aid creates a symbiotic relationship, where all people offer material goods or assistance to one another.

The phrase "centralized organization" may seem like a lot, but it doesn't have to be huge in the least. It's just a network of people all working to the betterment of themselves and their community. It is how humans lived for nearly all of the history that humans have existed in.

During COVID, many of us naturally fell back into that model. And many of us are doing so again, when infrastructure seems precarious. Do you have a circle of friends/family/loved ones in which everyone shows up to their capacity and their gifts are used? Think about it for a moment. Someone drives auntie to her appointments because she can't drive, but auntie cooks for everyone, while one of the nephews takes care of the dogs, and cousin Bertie swings by to drop off some produce from his vegetable patch. Linda mows the lawn, and then your neighbor across the street brings by blueberry muffins for everyone. That's a family, right? *And it's mutual aid.* Showing up in hyperlocal ways with a decentralized power structure is simple, and by using this approach you will see immediate impact with what you are trying to do.

You may be looking at all these options and thinking "yeah, but this is a larger community need that isn't being addressed yet, and an NPO will allow us to draw down funding to tackle it. I really think that's the appropriate structure." Fair enough. You can also look at how to fold into the NPO landscape without taking bigger, more complicated swings. Start by looking around with an eye toward collaboration.

- Are there any nonprofits doing similar work in other areas?

- If yes, can you start a chapter in your community?

- Is there an NPO doing similar work that you can fold your idea into?

  - If so, you may be able to convince them to provide fiscal sponsorship.

  - Another way to collaborate, depending on their own financial solvency, is to provide the other organization with a percentage of your incoming funding to move you under their umbrella.

- Both of these approaches will demonstrate to funders that you are working in collaboration instead of competition, while reducing overhead so more money goes to program services. All without having to jump through all the legal and fiscal hoops to prop up your program.

There are lots of ways of doing good outside the NFP market, or within it . . . but on smaller, more manageable terms, at least starting out.

So how do you start doing all that background work?

So much research. So much. But we got some good starting points for you.

Whether you are looking to start your own not-for-profit (or you are looking to get involved in one that already exists), Faith and Joe can safely say that when either of us regretted any level of involvement in the NFP world, the truth *was* out there—but we weren't looking and listening hard enough. We were excited about participating in a cause and didn't give enough thought to the underlying mechanisms. If we had researched the history of the organization or talked to former board members, we would have known exactly what dysfunctional dynamics we were getting involved in. Hell, most of the time you can tell if something is trouble simply by reading their newsletters and paying attention. And so much of the resources that you are going to need have already been collected for you.

- **Columbia University**, for example, has excellent resources on NFPs. (See References for the web address.) Not just professional NFP organizations and directories, but also how to find the financials and other data regarding an existing NFP and how to find funding of your own. They also have free ebooks on budgeting, financial management, and accounting.

- **The University of Rochester Library System** goes even harder, sharing basic terms and how they are operationalized in the nonprofit world, as well as similar information on how to learn more about financials and other information you need to understand and/or build your own NFP structure. (These are in the References section too.) Libraries, by the way? Excellent not-for-profits.

- **The Urban Institute (urban.org)** has a whole section of nonprofits and philanthropy data (some of which we use throughout this book to prove certain points). It also manages the National Center on Charitable Statistics as an open data platform.

- **ProPublica's Nonprofit Explorer** lets you browse the annual returns filed by nonprofits, letting you see their executive compensation, revenue, expenses, and the like (projects.propublica.org/nonprofits), which is another resource of data that we used within this book.

We would also suggest connecting with individuals working in programs with the same social goals you have. For example, when looking at starting a program in San Antonio, Faith and another local therapist met with the individuals running a successful program in Austin and got incredible advice from a group of people who were very generous with their time (collaboration!) because they wanted to see us succeed and were happy to share their hard-earned wisdom. Some of their shared wisdom shows up throughout this book, it was so valuable.

Once you've identified a like-minded program, ask if you can attend programming or board meetings or anything else that could help you see the inner workings of a program, especially one that is sized similarly to what your intended scale-up is.

And all of this will help you formulate strategies around getting your NFP up and running, while avoiding pitfalls you may witness or that other world-changers warn you about. And that is an excellent start.

Savior behavior

Speaking of pitfalls, here's a big one. Do you feel like your worth is tied to how much you are helping others? We're going to say this slowly and lovingly: it's too easy to fall into the mindset that you are helping people that are lower than you are in the hierarchy of the world. But, you protest, I *am* helping people! Yes, you may well be. But that doesn't make you any better than them. And more importantly, it likely doesn't make your ideas any better than theirs. It is incredibly likely that the population that you serve knows *exactly* how to utilize any resources that you have access to into methods for solving their problems.

This may seem like a small distinction. But it moves like a boulder. It's easy to get into the mindset that, because you are helping people, you are saving them from themselves. But you are helping to save them from emergencies, capitalism, or a lack of opportunities. The adage applies here that *some people didn't* make *good choices, they* had *good choices.* This applies more often than not in the nonprofit world. Most hungry people know exactly how to feed themselves just like most people feel guilty about not having more time in their day to exercise, but they still know how.

It bears stating that the mindset of "saving" someone else is inherently born of patriarchal, capitalist, white supremacy and the way that it infects thinking in Western society.

Years ago, an executive suggested that interns could receive bus passes and token benefits for their contributions to the organization. The board agreed that this sounded like a nice gesture, but Joe interrupted to say, "I think they would rather receive the small stipend instead, which would also require less work and oversight from us. If we are going to give them something, wouldn't it be better if they could spend it as they see fit? When I have received things like that, I either feel an obligation to use them or they sit in a drawer unspent." One person agreed vigorously until the room did. The problem was that the proposal was, once again, implying that the interns would ride the bus while the executives would not. To be fair, it was an offering of genuine kindness, but it wasn't tailored to the needs of the recipients.

In another example, a satellite grocery store opened up a block from the Microcosm office. Periodically staff would wander over to get snacks and treats. An employee asked for a chocolate bar. The cashier intoned: "Oh, we don't have those. We serve homeless people sometimes and we wouldn't want them to be tempted by a chocolate bar instead of some nice, fresh vegetables." Joe was proud when the employee responded, "A chocolate bar seems like useful calories for someone who doesn't have a stove; more than a head of raw kale does. Besides, sometimes you just want a chocolate bar after a long day." It's true that we can moralize against others' choices all day long, so you want to impose critical thinking on top of every decision. Is there a simpler way to achieve the goal?

An important aspect of escaping savior behavior is asking yourself if you are imposing on people with your offering. Are your actions going to require more time and labor on their part? Are you adding unnecessary steps to a process? Have you discussed the impact of your method on the affected beneficiaries of your work? It doesn't do anyone any good if they can't jump through the hoops. The best way to help someone is by not making the act about your own feelings.

Meeting the community's needs—by asking them what they need

And then the next part? The most important part? You need to ask the community you desire to serve *what they actually need.* We are going to discuss, later in this book, ways to simplify the process of assisting in meeting those needs with as few hoops to jump through as possible. But first you have to ask. Because you're doing this for them—not yourself—right? So shouldn't their needs always be centered in all of your core activities?

Faith was a grant evaluator for a partnership grant funded by Substance Abuse and Mental Health Services Agency (SAMHSA) that connected two groups of peer providers in Texas. SAMHSA said, "we're gonna give you a little bit of money to see what you can do to mobilize these forces into collaboration." So Faith designed an online survey and sent it out to the stakeholders with a request for them to pass it along to *their* stakeholders, a process referred to as "snowball sampling" or as a "chain referral sampling" plan. The idea was if people found the questions that were being asked useful, they would encourage others to complete the survey as well.

People did. Resoundingly. And gave us incredibly useful data regarding what their needs were. And a lot of that data surprised us by demanding a shift from what we thought the focus should be to what the community really was hoping to receive. The data led to us getting further funding to then go do those things. And we were asked to present the development of the tool itself to other SAMHSA grant recipients in hopes it could lend itself to dialogue in other communities.

It seemed like an outsized amount of attention at the time because it didn't occur to any of us that our approach was unusual.

If you want to help a community? Start by asking what help is needed. Of the actual people being served. Not community stakeholders. Not the local congresspeople. Not local business owners. I mean, fine, ask them, too. But center your activities around those needing help.

The real need should be spoken to by those who *have that need.*

THE INDIVIDUALS YOU SERVE COME FIRST

*E*very nonprofit needs to start by aligning its value chain. What does that mean? It means that you have to identify how you are moving money from the public to those that you aim to benefit, do so in the shortest path, and show how you are benefiting your clients. If you always prioritize those that you serve above all else, you can almost always simplify your workflow considerably, eliminate bureaucracy, and accomplish more with every dollar. Bonus: this will also result in the people that you serve speaking glowingly about how great your organization is. The opposite is also true.

Story time. An intern of Faith's was working at a not-for-profit that served unhoused women and their children. The program was funded through a local church, and my intern loved the work and loved seeing women regain their power. But Intern ran into a couple of problems. And the problems had to do with the way the women benefiting from this program were expected to "pay" for the support they were receiving.

The women were forced to volunteer at the church's charity shop, waiting on the parishioners that shop there as if they were dressers at a high-end department store. They were also made to attend services at the church that was funding the mission.

And we don't mean that they had to just go sit at the church service (which is ick enough, to our way of thinking); they were expected to give testimony to the congregation about how much the program was helping them and how well they were doing, etc.

These "payments" were designed to have members of the church community feel good about the money they were donating, by having those receiving the aid provide a level of emotional genuflection in return for their three-hots-and-a-cot.

Do you know who didn't feel good about this process? Intern and coworkers. And the women who were receiving the support. It was demeaning and fetishizing and honestly, just gross.

Intern went to the church board and suggested they maybe, you know, *not* demand charity recipient bootlicking—to no avail. When she told me about it, I went fully nuclear and scared their board attorney into submission . . . and was really only able to do so by pointing out that Texas HB 300 (also known as the Texas Medical Records Privacy Act) expanded the definition of *covered entitie*s in the state, making the members of this church board liable for non-authorized disclosures of protected health information.

They backed off immediately (and probably still hate me, which I love for us). But *only* because I had the law on my side, not because Intern and her Bitch-of-a-Board-Supervisor were making a solid case that they were shaming the very people they were purporting to help.

Making a difference in participants' lives is not the same thing as *centering services around the lived experiences of program participants.* We know you won't confuse the two, right?

Inequality researcher Lehn Benjamin noted that in more than fifty texts on nonprofit management, most had full chapters devoted to working with boards, staff, and volunteers . . . but not the program beneficiaries. Another text analysis she completed on outcome measurement guides showed that the NPOs couched program participants as targets of these interventions, and passive ones at that. Meaning that outcome measures may include the percentage of people who completed their GED with agency support, but no one asked questions like, "Did you like the program?" "Did you feel safe?" "Did you feel respected?" "Did anyone ask about and try to meet your personal needs?" The message, then, is clear. The GED matters, but the person obtaining it does not.

All strategies regarding the management of the organization should be centered around the participants' experience of the program. And throughout this book, we are going to go into depth about some of the ways of doing so. But "the why" regarding most of what we talk about will be abundantly clear the minute the experience of program participants is centered.

There is an adage in peer-led spaces that says, "nothing about us without us." And that adage should be true in all service-forward spaces. Do you want gratitude and devotion and the ego boost of helping someone? Or do you want those you serve to feel proud of their work and their accomplishments within your program because they reached out for the resources they needed to help themselves?

The people providing those direct services come next

If we are centering the experience of program participants as discussed in the previous section, one of the first things we have to do is make sure they have consistent and competent support. Staff burnout and staff turnover leads to worse outcomes for program participants and erodes their faith in the agency overall. If our priority is to be in service of program participants, then the people who are providing those services should be treated with substantive regard, right?

(Right.)

Faith's mom worked for the American Red Cross in the late 1980s and it was a horrible experience. She was good at the job itself, and she loved helping other military spouses, but she was expected to type all her documentation on a typewriter, and that documentation time did not count as hours worked. She was up all night taking crisis calls, trying to get information from military bases around the world. Then she was expected to document all of this work on my Brother typewriter. I have clear memories of her sobbing and typing through the night and into the wee hours of the morning—so I got curious about the payment structure for that organization, present-day.

So let's look. The President and CEO of the American Red Cross (ARC) is Gail McGovern. According to the 2023 ARC 990 filings, she made $819,082 in salary and another $13,1509 in "other compensation," which is presumably ARC's contributions to her health insurance, retirement matching, etc. Four other employees in her C-Suite are making over half a million a year, before even counting the other contributions being made on their behalf.

Now, ARC notes on their website that salaries are related to the living expenses of the area the position is tethered to. Which makes sense. And presumably Gail McGovern is located at headquarters in Washington, DC, which is an expensive place to reside. So Faith went to the ARC website and looked up job listings in the DC area. None were entry-level, but by using a salary from somewhere with a lower cost of living rate Faith could demonstrate the least-to-most split without being sus.

Most of the DC-located jobs were executive level jobs. Cuz hey, it's the mother ship, which is also to be expected. Faith can bend over backwards to be fair (she *is* a yoga teacher after all).

The one DC job that wasn't a VP or Director role offered in July 2025 was titled "Principal, IT Disaster Recovery," which the job posting itself refers to as *mission critical*. The job is to test operation feasibility so ARC can deploy and provide aid successfully. You are expected to have both IT experience, statistical analysis experience, and disaster recovery design and testing experience. All relevant degrees and certifications are also required or strongly encouraged. The salary range is $90K-$100K and is not bonus eligible

(Ms. McGovern received a $50K signing bonus when she took the job in 2008).

This disaster recovery IT position seems like a vital role requiring (understandably) extensive experience. In an expensive city. What is considered a middle-class income in the DMV (DC-Maryland-Virginia) area? According to CNBC in 2023 (two years before that particular job posting), it is $221,000.

Now, does Ms. McGovern deserve the salary she is making? We know there are plenty of arguments out there that she does. We may even agree with some of them.

But shouldn't the information technology rock star who is designing the systems that allow the American Red Cross to deploy in disasters and supply assistance also deserve a livable salary commensurate with their experience? We think there are just as many, if not more, arguments to be made on their behalf.

Please understand we are not making an argument against paying the C-suite of nonprofits commensurate with their experience. We are making the argument that *all* positions should be adequately compensated, not just commensurate with their experience but also using the reasoning that if people are working full time, they should be able to pay their bills. Especially if working for an organization as flush as the American Red Cross.

Because your next question, surely, is maybe they can't afford to pay their disaster recovery IT people well. The answer? The expenses reported in their 990 filing for 2023 was $2.97B. Their revenue was $3.22B. They turned a profit. They can afford it.

And, okay. The American Red Cross is easy to pick on. They're huge. And they made Faith's mom cry.

But it is also a clear example of a systemic problem. Because ARC is *not* a scam program— and scam programs are a whole other ball of wax.

According to an FBI report on internet crime, Americans lost $4.4 million to charity fraud . . . a number that doesn't even include the emergence of fake online fundraisers which are almost impossible to even estimate. And ARC isn't a fraudulent charity. ARC is a four-star charity with a 100% rating from Charity Navigator, and they *do* provide services across the globe. Ms. McGovern isn't a scam artist pocketing donations. Nevertheless, this agency is not prioritizing the employees in service provider and mission critical roles. And we can do better.

Nothing about us without our employees

Let's broaden the lens instead of continuing to pick on the American Red Cross. Let's look at the data around nonprofit staffing trends in general.

The National Council on Nonprofits conducted a survey on hiring and retaining staff and found that Joe and Faith aren't fussing about nothing.

Almost three-quarters of the nonprofit agency directors surveyed reported having current job vacancies, and nearly the same number of respondents noted that the unfilled jobs are service delivery positions, programming positions, and sundry entry-level positions. The agencies providing direct services also noted that their waitlist for services has increased. Why? Almost three-fourths of the respondents again noted that they can't compete with other salaries in the area when it comes to recruiting and retaining employees. Nor can they cope with the pile-on of stress and burnout due to the overloaded working conditions.

When asked about possible solutions, the obvious mentions are better funding. But people also suggested things like subsidized child care and better student loan forgiveness for staff so they could afford to continue working.

Now. We agree that both of these things should be readily available . . . for *everyone*. But agency directors stating it is what they need to survive is a frustratingly circular logic that does not address their role in supporting the current structural problem here. They are charitable organizations asking the government to provide charity *to their staff* so they can afford to keep their jobs that provide charity *to their recipients*. Make it make sense, because it doesn't.

We don't have things like expanded subsidized child care in the US and we are not even close to getting those things. And as someone who has worked at qualifying agencies, Faith can tell you that if you are banking on student loan forgiveness? Don't. Of the four *million* Public Service Loan Forgiveness (PSLF) applications processed between September 2020 and June 2023, only 2.4% met their eligibility and only .5% actually got loan forgiveness. Which is actually *down* from the pre-2020 percentage of 1%.

So instead of needing to subsidize the salaries of employees with government or other outside funding . . . we just need to pay employees a living wage to begin with. That's true for any full-time job in any sector (and should it need to be explicated . . . we are not accepting arguments against common decency). And if it is especially true anywhere? The people who are in these really tough jobs with tough hours providing care to individuals in desperate need of support? They come first.

Now, we know there are plenty of amazing programs running on an absolute shoe-string. In these programs, no one is getting paid *anything* and everyone is volunteering whatever time they have because they believe in the work. And the founders make sure their staff get paid first as they expand. And there are others who are running programs and paying their employees *from their own pockets* because they are financially able to do so and believe in the work and giving back.

José Andrés' World Central Kitchen (a place to which Faith donates regularly) is another large-scale international charity.[9] José Andrés doesn't

---

9 And yes, this is the organization that had seven team members who were murdered in Gaza in 2024 . . . and went

make a single dime from his own organization. He is listed on their 990 filing as the Founder and Chief Food Officer with a salary of zero dollars and zero cents. At every level we have people doing good and important work because it needs to be done.

We are not coming for *any* of them. We know a lot of y'all personally and adore you greatly. The rescue cat currently sitting next to Faith as she types this thanks one program founder in particular for their service.

However, "believing in the work" is also a constant refrain said to individuals who are working full-time and trying to live on that money. And they are getting the message that complaining means you don't care about the mission. And what happens? Exactly what the survey cited above says. Positions stay unfilled, turnover is ridiculous, and service to the community suffers exponentially.

---

right back to fighting to be allowed back in to feed people.

Mitigate power by reducing income disparity

In 2025, Joe's income from Microcosm is less than $10,000 per year, and Joe remains the lowest paid employee in the organization. Why? Joe is more focused on the initial goals of the project, so Joe created a simplified lifestyle to compensate. This isn't right for everyone, because it's a series of compromises. But life is a series of compromises. It's also quite a bit easier to negotiate what you need from your staff if your salary doesn't put you in a higher tax bracket than theirs does.

In 1997, Faith worked as a case manager for a program providing services to new teen moms. It was a lot of parenting skills training and case management. The program was a United Way funded agency, with a mission to prevent child abuse. Faith had a bachelor's degree as well as the specific certification this role required, and as a new mother herself, a strong belief in the work she was doing.

Faith (she loves writing about herself in third person like this), was making $18,000 a year. In today's dollars that translates to just under $28,000 a year, according to the Measuring Worth website, a service that measures relative worth over time. The executive director of the agency (who did not have a college degree or the aforementioned certification) was making $45,000. This was a secret at the time because it was so much more than the rest of us, but Faith saw it on the fax machine one day. How much does this translate into 2025 dollars? Just under $90K.

Now, that's a solid income in South Texas, especially for someone without the education and experience of the individuals working there—while Faith, on her salary, was receiving food stamps and WIC and desperately cobbling together child care, the same as her clients were. Yes, thirty years later she is still salty about it. During her time there, people came and left in droves, and on top of these other indignities she was forever getting new caseloads and longer hours and trying desperately to keep the families she served afloat, while keeping herself and her baby afloat, too.

It is unsurprising that she also ended up leaving, creating more harm to the families who desperately needed the services she provided.

This is more common than not, but it isn't universal. As a board supervisor for newly-licensed professional counselors, Faith worked with several people who ended up working for a local organization that serves veterans and their families. Many stayed on with the agency long after they gained the experience and skills that would allow them to get many other opportunities in the field.

Why? The pay from this program is not just competitive to the market, it's *good*. When the program was founded, they made the decision to match what the VA itself pays their clinicians, which is much higher than the market average. Many of them are single parents who have been able to buy a home and pay for their kids' football cleats and other sundry needs. They aren't wealthy but they have good pay, solid benefits, and a work-life balance.

And when thinking about this, Faith looked up this program's 990 and found out that the C-suite is also *very* well compensated. And this time she isn't salty about it, because the staff has their basic needs accounted for so they can focus on the mission.

If you are scaling in the direction of having full-time staff, plan for this from the get-go. Build out a budget that accommodates your staff to have salaries that they can live on. If you need to build and expand slowly to do so, it's still the better long-term strategy.

An Urban Institute report that found that most nonprofits choose to cut salaries and benefits long before scaling back their operations. But as we saw from the previously cited research, operations end up suffering anyway, with long waitlists and overwork of the remaining staff until they end up leaving as well. Prioritizing the clients really does mean prioritizing those who directly serve the clients.

And it is fiscally responsible in the long-term as well. You should look at the market rate and line-item out reasonable salaries when applying for funding from the get-go. Cite the following if need be, from The Nonprofit Center at La Salle University:

> The cost of replacing a single employee can range from 50% to d/+ over 400% of their annual salary, depending on the position and complexity of the role.

Even if client wait-times and break-downs in service provision is less of a concern, even if taking care of the people who are caring for the clients the program serves is less of a concern? Can't we agree that everyone expects you to be fiscally responsible? This is part of showing them you are. The research is already done for you!

Take Action!

- How many part- and full-time staff does your current capacity require?

- What is a reasonable expectation for your annual budget for salaries?

- How does this compare to your current budget for salaries?

- Where will these numbers be in another three years at your current growth trajectory?

- How does your organization's budget grow as your staffing needs do?

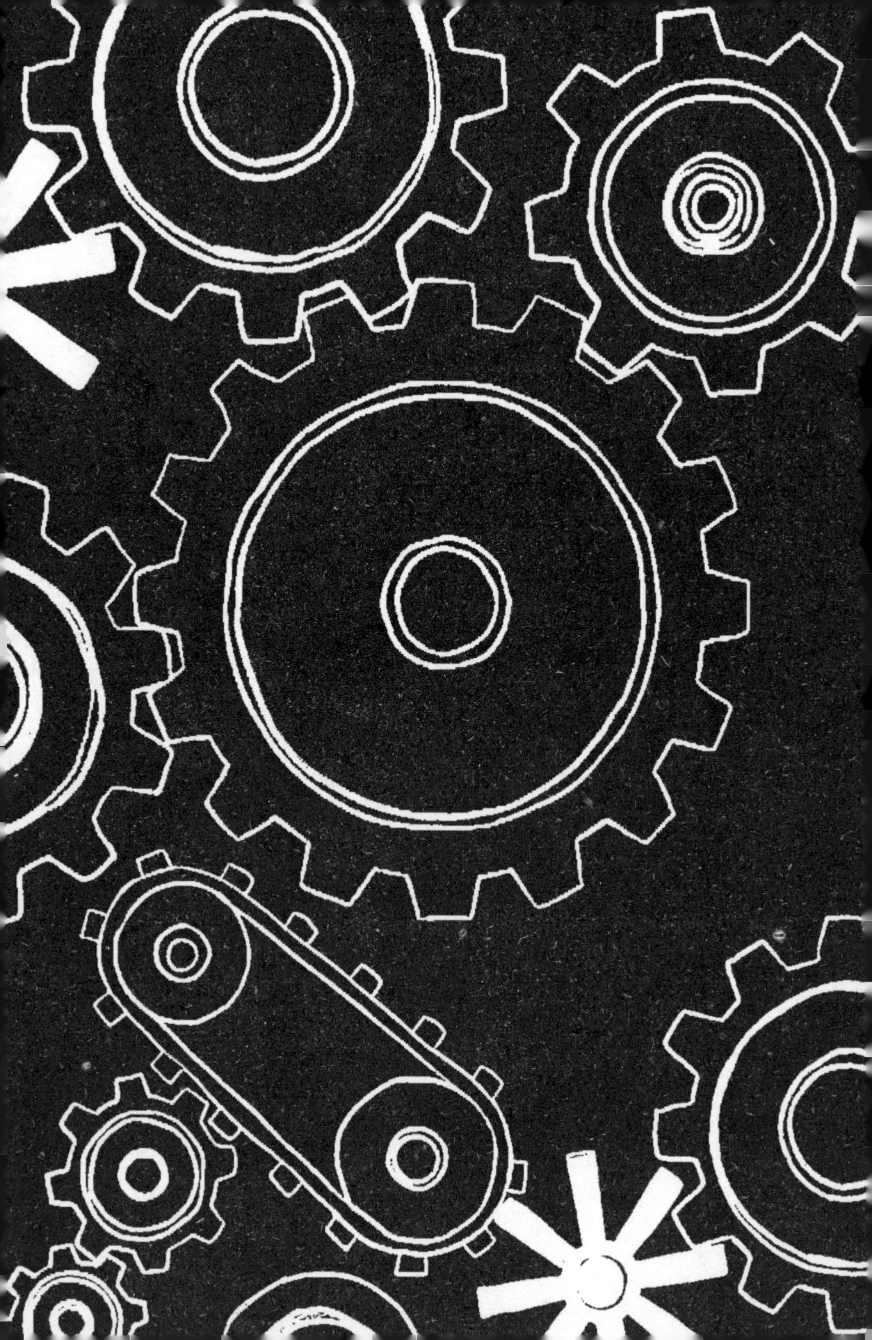

IF PEOPLE ASK FOR HELP? HELP THEM. FFS.

In other words, means testing is the worst

So this section is where we drag *means testing* for filth. Means testing refers to any kind of formula that is used to determine a participant's eligibility for a program. It almost always involves establishing what income and assets potential program participants have, meaning: "We won't help you unless you are super poor and prove your super-poorness."

This is also what we refer to as *morality means testing,* where there is a determination of your good moral character before allowing you assistance. You can't just be poor, you have to demonstrate you are the right kind of poor. Deservingly poor. To give a few examples: You can't demonstrate any spending on anything fun ever. You may have to go to our church (fun fact: Jesus would *never*). You have to demonstrate that there are no drugs in your system. Whatever.

First of all, means testing is a whole-ass waste of money, which the proponents of this level of gatekeeping deny by using very sneaky math. Matt Bruenig, founder of People's Policy Project, has written extensively on the topic and is smarter than us about it so you should definitely go read his work at *Jacobin*. He demonstrates how taxation is hidden as phase-outs in federal funding . . . *and* that when you look at overhead cost savings you are actually able to provide *more* direct support. In short, it costs less to offer *universal benefits* than to test everyone who asks for them.

Better yet, Bruenig cleverly shows what others missed: that changing the timing of when a benefit is taxed can double the positive financial impacts of an NPO's programs. The way these benefits and taxes are currently applied *reduces their effectiveness.* The way the fees are categorized hides the true costs. These federally funded programs would be more effective if they were evaluated simply by comparing total costs to total benefits. Instead, they keep on with this game of three-card monte ... playing with your fucking tax dollars.

And the morality component?

It's bad enough that religious organizations make participation in their faith a requirement to receive aid. You know what we mean ... the places that have a food pantry which opens after a prayer service that you have to attend if you want that jar of peanut butter. But a big one that many people, especially government representatives, adore that is just stupidly expensive? Drug testing.

Joe and Faith love to Godzilla-stomp the narrative that individuals receiving cash assistance (Temporary Aid for Needy Families [TANF], also known as welfare) use drugs at disproportionate rates to the rest of the country, and that by denying them benefits we are only protecting them from themselves and from wasting our tax dollars. Please put on your stompiest boots and join us, yeah?

Labor writer Joe Mayall, in his article "Means Testing Welfare is ALWAYS Dumb," demonstrated (with an enjoyable level of verve and snark) how fucking stupid those programs always turn out to be, using several examples, including the four-month shit show that discreetly[10] happened in Florida.

In 2011, in their quest to make Texas and Oklahoma look politically moderate, Florida passed a law requiring all TANF recipients to pass a drug test. The law didn't last long because it is deeply unconstitutional, and the ACLU had it repealed. But during the four months it was active, 4,086 applicants were tested and 2.6% tested positive for an illicit substance.

------

10 While it's not difficult to morally mislead the public into believing in drug testing the recipients of public benefits, the costs and rewards of doing so were not divulged—or seemingly even researched by Florida. It was sort of a "trust us, we know what we're doing" type of situation.

And yes, that actually *is* disproportionate from the general population. A federal report, also from 2011, found that 8.32% of Floridians used illicit substances. So that means that TANF applicants were 320% *less* likely to use drugs than non-recipients.[11]

This isn't rocket science. Drugs are fucking expensive and the people applying for TANF are broke as hell.

How much money was saved by the state by denying those 2.6% of folks who popped hot? The denied benefits saved Florida $73,140. Too bad the testing cost $118,140, I guess?

So taxpayers dropped $45K in four months in the name of faux indignation. People who owned stock in drug testing companies did well, though—including the sitting governor of Florida at the time (Rick Scott), who owned $62 million in stock of one such company.

---

11 During a press conference, Aasif Mandvi asked Governor Rick Scott if he would subject himself to drug testing since he also receives public funds. It's on YouTube. Thing of beauty.

Stomp. Stomp.

And if any program cares about cost savings? Now you have plenty of proof that means testing grinds cost savings into sand.

But it's not just the money, right? We are wanting to design programs around participant-centered thinking. Meaning the people we serve experience their own lives and the needs we are there to help meet. Second of all, forced humiliation through drug testing is not participant-centered thinking. And we already agreed that any program that we are involved with needs to center those receiving services.

(This is us presuming that if you have gotten this far into the book instead of setting it on fire, you are in agreement with our new world order thinking.)

Yes, we totally understand that you want to make sure that the people who really need the help get the help. And we have plenty of data from government assistance programs that show that even the people who would truly qualify *are less likely to actually apply* because of all the hoops and barriers associated with accessing services. Like our friend Matt Bruenig at the People's Policy Project points out, this complex system then fails to serve the people we stated we are there to serve, and it cuts the legs out from under the intended effects of receiving that support (reducing poverty, in this case).

Jumping through hoops is poor exercise

To give a counter example, Social Security and at least some components of Medicare are a universal benefit to Americans once you reach a certain age. (The components that are not universal, Medicare Parts A and D, are means tested.) It's not a perfect system; you still have to apply, and not everyone gets the same amount. But the uptake rates of individuals accessing and utilizing their benefits is near universal: 97% for Social Security and 96% for Medicare. It does not matter if you are someone's Tia on the southside or a Rockefeller. Once you are a senior, you can access that benefit.

But what about other services, ones that are means tested and can be accessed only by those living significantly below the poverty level? For those, the access and uptake numbers drop. Only 85% of the individuals who qualify for food stamps receive them, as an example. And that number drops to 75% for the working poor, because proving that they are *still fucking poor* is complicated and time consuming and they are *trying to go to work.*

The Earned Income Tax Credit also has a lower participation rate. The idea is supposed to be that if you have a job but your income is below a certain amount (and taking into consideration factors like how many kids you have), then you receive a tax deduction. But because only 78% percent of those who qualify have been able to jump through the necessary hoops to receive the benefit, the poverty-reducing effect is also reduced. And *that* means that the effectiveness of the policy is only half (possibly less) than expected.

There are all these hoops that people have to jump through. Then the hoops keep moving.

Then they get set on fire. And it's exhausting, and they give up.

And this is all just the people who qualify under very rigid standards. You have to be very, very, very broke to be considered living at the poverty level. There are plenty of others who are also stuck in cycles of poverty that are making a little more than that, and therefore don't qualify under these guidelines.

Now here is the moral part of the argument. Study after study has demonstrated that the process of applying for benefits is humiliating. And anxiety provoking. People gather up the courage to ask for help, then are expected to jump through hoops and have every facet of their existence inspected. And they are treated with suspicion. And even contempt.

And they are unsure how that same information is being used and stored and shared with others, which is of increasing concern in recent times.

And *then* a good portion of them are told they do not qualify for help because they make twenty dollars too much a month, or some equally ridiculous measure.

People who are courageous enough to ask for the help they need to put their lives back together should receive that help. Period. And be treated with respect for doing so. Vulnerability is hard work, and they are making an effort for their lives (and often the lives of their families) to get better.

Are there people out there who are gaming the system and are just going to suck up all the free shit they can get? Sure. But, for example, benefits fraud hovers around 0.14%—that's well below 1%![12] Why? The process is time-consuming and exhausting, even without stupid hoops to clear. Most people, if they have fifty dollars, will just go buy the groceries. Not wait in line for hours at the food bank. Hell, most people, if they only have twenty dollars, will find a way to make it work rather than request assistance.

By and large, the people who ask for assistance fucking need it. Help them.

---

12 sgp.fas.org/crs/misc/R45147.pdf

And help them as directly as possible

The U.S. has a culturally embedded value system around our need to be independently successful. Toxic hyper-independence isn't just a trait of those of us who experienced childhood trauma—it's also apparently the American way.

According to studies cited in Annie Lowrey's book on universal basic income, *Give People Money*, the World Values Survey and Pew Research have both demonstrated that we tend to think that poverty and need are entirely our own damn fault. We are far more likely to think systemic issues are about our choices and/or lack of effort (hustle culture! Boss babe! Rise and grind! ETFUCKINGCETERA), where citizens in European companies view poverty as an almost inescapable trap replete with corruption that can only be mitigated with connections and luck.

At a rally hosted by AFL-CIO leadership in San Antonio a few years ago (Faith saw Bernie Sanders speak and is salty about how he appears to be in much better shape than she is while being

873 years older than her), one of the labor leaders reminded the crowd: "We aren't looking for a handout. We are hard workers and like working for a living, we just want to be able to actually live on the fruits of our labor." Same idea. Americans take pride in being harder workers and value earning our way.

Ms. Lowrey shared these statistics in support of other data that demonstrates that infusions of cash into people's lives don't impact the labor market nearly to the extent as one may suspect. We share it because we think it serves as an appropriate framework for understanding the profound discomfort people have with direct help.

Give People Money also should be required reading for anyone working in the NFP field, because Lowrey demonstrates time and again that direct action is the better and more cost-efficient plan by showing how different programs have succeeded or failed in making demonstrable positive changes in the lives people live within the communities they live in.

(For example, she shows how the donated Toms Shoes end up providing rafter insulation in homes because they aren't climate appropriate to actually wear . . . while objectively small cash assistance provided by GiveDirectly.org[13] [and only once, not regularly like Universal Basic Income would be] made demonstrable and long-lasting differences that could quite literally be seen from space. Satellite images have been used to see how people's homes and surrounding areas change after receiving this no-strings-attached money.) Now, it sounds well and good to say things like "I donate thousands of shoes to impoverished nations per year." But do you think that if Toms asked the people that they were donating shoes to for feedback, these shoes would end up on people's feet instead of as ceiling insulation? It's easy to be a critic. It's more difficult and important to do better within your own organization.

---

13 GiveDirectly.org has delivered $900M+ to 1.7M people living in poverty with no strings attached since 2009. By sending money directly to people who need it most, you eliminate the bureaucratic general and administrative expenses of most nonprofits.

What exactly is direct action?

Direct action, in this context, is the simple act of addressing the problem yourself, instead of throwing money into a bottomless pit of an organization where 70–91% of your donation goes to feed general and administrative costs.[14] Direct action looks to eliminate infrastructure needed to achieve the goal. (In other words, with minimal hoops to jump through, and fuck means testing in the ear.)

Twenty five years ago, Joe worked for a nonprofit that fed people lunch as part of educational programming. Local restaurants and grocery stores donated food and it was used to create a lunch spread. The system was convoluted, with people cooking based on what they received each day. The food was carefully portioned and plated so everyone got the right amount. This consumed hours of resources each day. Joe simplified the process by asking what the donations were from the restaurants, and selecting matching groceries

---

14 One nonprofit was found to have used only 6% of funds raised on their actual programs. Where did the rest go? latimes.com/archives/la-xpm-2000-dec-31-mn-6753-story.html

that would be good pairings, spreads, and sauces to make the food more appetizing. One person needed to pick up the donations and put them on a table with cutlery in a suggestive manner. Everyone could plate and feed themselves. People were responsible enough to determine the size of their own portion. No cooking was needed.

To give another example that feels even more obvious, a nonprofit employee created an idea to benefit a charity but was worried about personal tax implications. Joe created a contract where the money moved directly from the benefactor to the charity and made the contract clear that this was not income for anyone else.

Over time, it is in the nature of almost any organization to become increasingly bloated. Orgs build out departments and add executive assistants and hire more people as they become busier and more successful to show just how successful they are. Sometimes funding is contingent upon adding jobs in response. Soon, they're adding offices and buildings and computers and an HR department to manage them all. The trouble is that, as anything grows, it's increasingly difficult to manage the output and efficiency of various departments. Worse, it's harder to manage the same culture across different departments and know who is being worked to the bone and who doesn't have enough to do. As funding dries up and times change, organizations need to restructure—and we don't mean this to read "layoffs." We mean "reshuffle the work so that one person isn't just checking another's work. At the point that one person's job is just to micromanage others, you need to restructure." As you grow, give an honest eye on how to reshape workflows to involve fewer people doing less work. You'd be amazed how rare this is. One friend who works for a Fortune 500 estimated that his office is doing work about 30% of the time. This is not uncommon.

In 2020, 80% of the staff of Microcosm began working from home. We always had a flexible rule that you could work from home if you wanted, but everyone preferred coming to work, as was the culture of the time. But in 2020, people started moving out of state and we started hiring more people from out of state. Before long, the offices that once housed eleven people working at desks were empty every day. So we began using them for storing empty boxes for the warehouse, to have meetings, and as a break room. We looked at the infrastructure we had and reshuffled it. I cannot tell you how many times an organization will let it slip that they have 8,000 square feet of unused office space that they pay for every month.

So. When it comes to direct action, the idea is to help whomever asks for help (with minimal hoops to jump through, and fuck means testing in the ear), and help them as directly as possible, while keeping administrative costs to a minimum.

Direct action could be as simple as moving the funds directly from the source to the recipient, handing food to hungry people, letting someone stay with you that has nowhere to go, or graffiting a giant penis around each pothole that you want the city to repair.[15] The world is your oyster, and once

15 Or, in the case of Portland Anarchist Road Care, fixing potholes themselves, which also motivated the city to take

you begin demonstrating the positive outcome of direct actions like this, it's easy to receive news coverage and attract like-minded people to help.

Especially with programs aimed at alleviating poverty and issues related to poverty. If people need food or jobs, the best way to manage either need is to give them money and trust them to know their circumstances, in both the short- and long-term, better than you do.

This seems obvious on the surface, if you are from a culture that recognizes poverty as a far more insidious form of quicksand than anything that showed up to attack Princess Buttercup in *The Princess Bride.* But if you are from a culture that views poverty as a moral failing you need to work your way out of? We are far less trusting of people's intentions and follow-through. Because by being poor they have demonstrated failure at doing so, right?

And then we are perpetuating the cycles of

poverty we are purporting to alleviate by staying in a paternalistic mindset about who knows best.

Take this example of an individual in the Midwest whose identity Faith is going to great lengths to hide. She (Midwest lady, not Faith) was tasked to start a program to improve the health of older women living in a significantly impoverished area, and she used the money to start some kind of awareness campaign[16] about how it is important to get exercise and encouraged people to do more

---

16 The whole idea of awareness campaigns comes from a model introduced in the 1980s known as the Information Deficit Model. The idea is that if people have the information they need, they will make the choices we deem they should make. Faith would like to write about twenty pages about why that is about the stupidest thing you should focus your charity work on, but you'll have to accept the 192 pages we already wrote about this in one of our other books, *How to be Accountable*. Spoiler alert: information does no such thing and just as often backfires. The literature is replete with failures of awareness campaigns, but one of the most significant in recent years was the awareness campaign about the HPV vaccine in the U.S. The campaign made the vaccine a hot-button issue, and it was decried by some as granting permission for promiscuous behavior. Before the campaign, 90% of preteens of any gender received the vaccine; after the shit show, only 33% of girls and 7% of boys got the vaccine.

walking. This was as embarrassing a failure as one might expect.

The neighborhood in question was pretty dangerous and not particularly walkable. Additionally, many of these women had jobs that kept them on their feet for most of their waking hours. What would happen if they were just given money toward the goal of becoming healthier? Maybe they use it to join a local inexpensive gym. Maybe they use it to augment their grocery budget and buy foodstuffs that better support their individual health needs. Maybe they use the money to pay the copay on their prescriptions so they are not having to hoard their insulin and take half-doses between paychecks.

Maybe they use it for something that is not directly in support of any of those goals, but it alleviates the mental bandwidth tax that poverty creates, thereby freeing up their mental space and diminishing their stress response. (Lowrey covers this, too, in *Give People Money*. Turns out that the brain fog caused by living in constant poverty and distress is akin to losing 13 IQ points.) Because maybe they have a grandbaby that needs a twenty dollar gym uniform so they are no longer flunking gym because they can't dress out. Or they need period products. Or they need to fix their car, allowing them to take a better paying job outside the bus route.

People don't need "information campaigns," they need help. One nonprofit was formed with the sole purpose of funding billboards that used Joe's slogan "Punk rock saved my life"—but Joe instead had to have the difficult talk with the proprietor that this wasn't a constructive campaign. The campaign seemingly was focused on the idea that this phrase would profoundly touch anyone who saw it in a life-changing way, similar to drug and alcohol recovery campaigns. But a lack of punk rock isn't the disconnect in people's lives; they were disconnected from other needs. The founder came to Joe to ask to fund a billboard campaign, who was not interested. The campaign didn't center the individuals served; the founder literally wanted to include photos of herself.

There are so many other programs that are not designed with a primary goal of the alleviation of poverty through resource allocation. But there are also many orgs that *do* center alleviating problems through resource allocation. One that Faith uses regularly is called Watch Duty. The Watch Duty app is a 503(c)(3) nonprofit that lets you know if there are fires in your area. The Watch Duty app isn't insisting Faith go through a fire awareness training program to use the app. They don't think she needs to fight the fires herself. Both of these things would have minimal utility in her life, or in service of their mission. She's just trying to track environmental issues that affect her breathing substantially. Expecting her to do anything else in service of the information she needs is just as dumb as a "walking for your health" awareness program in a dangerous neighborhood is.

People know. People know what they need. And they will surprise you far more often than not by taking care of business exceptionally well if you help them gain that access and trust them to follow through.

Take Action!

- What is the easiest and simplest path (remember that simple and easy are two different things!) from where you are to the services that you want to provide? Write out the steps.

- How can you simplify the process for the people that you are trying to help?

- How and when will you know to reassess and restructure this workflow?

- How can you better simplify the process for your beneficiaries?

- How can you better involve the beneficiaries of your work into the decision making process of how they receive services?

- How could your efforts be *perceived* as morally judging your beneficiaries?

DEMONSTRATE REAL IMPACT

*M*ost of the time, the data insights that NPOs are most interested in is donor data. They want to know who gave them money, how much, and at what intervals—to determine how to motivate them to give *more*. If you search for info on the topic, most Top Five lists about charity data problems will list at least three items about donor data. And usually the entirety of the list is about donor data strategies. But, honestly, there are way bigger problems.

Faith and Joe don't give a fuck about optimizing donor data, when no one even has good program efficacy data. Because—hot take? Stomp

stomp?—you can optimize donations if you are demonstrating program efficacy.

Data is difficult

Nonprofit Hub—a community hub for nonprofits—and EveryAction—a software platform for fundraising, advocacy, and donor management[17]—partnered in 2016 on a report looking at how 467 nonprofits are collecting and using their data . . . and? It's disheartening as fuck.

First off, they note that 90% of the responding agencies stated they sometimes or always tracked data. And we are as curious as you are, but the report didn't differentiate between the always and sometimes numbers . . . because, sometimes? What the fuck does sometimes mean? And the other 10% are DOING WHAT NOW?

And this was as good as this "State of Data" report got. Forty-eight percent of the

---

17 These aren't AI-embedded em dashes. We are Gen Xers and love a good em dash. We promise we write terribly all on our own.

respondents stated they didn't know all the ways their organization was tracking data, despite the fact that the respondents were individuals in leadership positions. Only 5% of the respondents stated that all of their decisions are data driven. The other 95% are apparently comfortable (at least a good chunk of the time) with . . . just vibes?

The Nonprofit Technology Network partnered with Idealware, a 501(c)(3) nonprofit that helps other nonprofits choose software that best meets their resource needs, to survey nonprofits, and they got more information on the data NPOs were tracking. Of the ones that were, 89% were tracking financial data. Meaning that donor info was their priority. Only half (50% exactly) were tracking program participant outcomes, and even less (41%) were looking at external data that would be relevant to their program goals and interests.

Joe has a friend who is a data analyst for nonprofits who is routinely asked to show their boss' *desired outcome* in the data, rather than being asked what the data shows.

(This is called lying, by the way.)

If the corporate world operated this way (and yeah, it sometimes does), the public would rebel against it. The difference is that if you allege that your nonprofit operates within the "public good," then the public curiously gives a lot more leeway and less criticism . . . though that's changing, too. Read on.

We all want to present our program in the most positive light. And the data chaos and the resulting holes in vital measures of program success create a problem far more common that most of us realize. Laura Quinn, the executive director of Idealware, is quoted in an article at CommunityForce that it is fairly standard practice for agency representatives to make up data they don't have. She estimated that a good *half* of the operating NPOs do this fairly regularly. She does go on to explain that it's usually because they never captured any specifics about whatever the point in question was, rather than just egregious lies about program efficacy.

(Though that definitely exists too. And while data on how frequently it happens doesn't exist, a sampling of posts on r/nonprofit demonstrates it happens fairly frequently and is awfully difficult to prove. Both the general public and donors large and small have noticed.)

And here is the "read on" mentioned earlier. The Donor Trust Report conducted by Give. org in 2025 found that 32% of their respondents trust charities less than they did five years ago. Seventy-three percent of respondents rated the importance of trusting a charity at a 9 or a 10 on a 10-point scale . . . and only 20% of those same survey participants stated they felt that level of trust in charities. A global survey reported by *Fast Company* stated that 60% of people worldwide said they don't have faith that nonprofits can accomplish their missions, and one-third of Americans don't trust charities to spend their money well.

If you look up articles on tracking NFP data you will find that almost all of the pieces out there focus on donation data, and how to make sure you are getting the most money out of your donors. And yes, staying afloat is important. But one of the best ways to keep donors invested, in our egregiously non-humble opinions, is to *demonstrate program efficacy.*

Donors are watching. Data published by *The NonProfit Times* found that if an NPO isn't transparent with their data, they receive 47% less in contributions than the organizations that are proactive about data sharing with the general public.

But you can't be transparent with data you don't have in the first place. Salesforce.org (the nonprofit arm of Salesforce.com, which provides tools for efficacious data tracking to NPOs, including some well-known programs like Make-A-Wish and St. Jude's) found that 76% of NFP respondents admitted to still needing to develop a data strategy for their organization, and 72% agreed that doing so is an expectation of these aforementioned donors, stating donors expect remote access to performance metrics about the agency. The 2017 "Foundation Reporting Study" by Social Solutions asked donors what information they most want to see, and by far the biggest reported desire (88% of respondents) was program outcomes.

If we want to do good work? And we want people to invest in that work? We have to do it through radical honesty. As Sir Terry Pratchett said in *The Science of Discworld*, "Science is not about building a body of known 'facts.' It is a method for asking awkward questions and subjecting them to a reality-check, thus avoiding the human tendency to believe whatever makes us feel good."

How to demonstrate it

Data is important. This is what helps us figure out our wins (for replication) and our opportunities for growth. Programs that didn't get the expected turnout or the expected results? We own that, fully, with a plan for improvement. That is how we rebuild trust with the public that both utilizes and funds us.

Orgs have a tendency to obfuscate this stuff and hide it on page 59 of the mandatory public reporting. To be fair, this is usually because of a discomfort with numbers, capacity overwhelm, or regular disorganization, but it still comes across as shady. And we are aiming for the opposite of shady. So it's better to know the data about how you are effective, how you could streamline, and how you will be more effective in the future.

And data is hard if that isn't your jam. Faith has a research PhD and has managed data for community agencies and nonprofits. Joe is an autodidact data nerd who dates a journalist and learns something new every day. Which is all to say, we love this shit, but recognize that's kinda rare. And we fully recognize that it can feel incredibly overwhelming if numbers make you itchy.

Faith has worked at community programs where managing data was one of her tasks. She has also been a data analyst on a NFP grant that carved out the funds to make sure that happened and happened well. She knows that it can otherwise be quite expensive for smaller organizations to do themselves.

Here's a little pep talk though.

Statistics is absolutely about logic, not math. The only time Faith ever had to complete complex statistical equations to understand the mechanisms behind them was in her first (of *five*) research classes in her PhD program. She vaguely remembers the a-ha moment of understanding how it works, and then never did it again. You never need to unless you also have dissertation-related psychosis. If you're good at logic, computers are great at math . . . so let the computer have at it.

Most of the numbers will be what we call *descriptive* statistics. These are just the numbers that describe what you're doing. The number of people who accessed services, what services were provided, etc. You don't have to do much with those numbers but report them. Whip up some averages, maybe, but that's no big.

Program efficacy can get a little trickier, but you can still do more than you'd expect on a small budget. Both of us have met with program developers and helped them, before they started, figure out what they were trying to measure and what data to collect in order to do so. The data input was done by support staff and handed back to us to run the statistical analysis, which was all of a five minute job. And many of the tools we used to measure differences were available online or in a regular Excel spreadsheet.

If you aren't sure where to start, look at other charities in your area that have great data game and find out how. Maybe you can partner with them and share resources, if they have a data nerd on staff. Someone, somewhere in your community is a Faith or a Joe.

Be transparent with program participants too

Another point that you will have to consider and build into the culture of your program is transparency with program participants. Remember we talked about being participant-centered? Here we go again. If you want real data from program participants they need to know exactly how it is going to be used and what details about their lives and experiences will be shared. As someone who was constantly needing to collect clinical data in community mental health settings, the best way Faith found to obtain consent was to frame this as *her* report card, rather than the program participants'. *You came in asking for help? Did we do our jobs and help?*

This is another place where partnering with other agencies can come in handy. Maybe you are one of four programs in the area that provides services to at-risk teen moms, and you share information with each other. For example, maybe there is an issue with families making their one-year Medicaid dental appointments, which puts their continued Medicaid coverage at risk. So the metric falls short of what funders expected.

The radical honesty part, then, is in the plan you have to fix it.

In this case, it might look something like this: "While our numbers varied from agency to agency, we all fell short in ensuring all of the teen families made the pediatric dental appointment required by Medicaid. Families cited struggles with finding in-network pediatric dentists that were taking new patients. Our agency outreach coordinator set up a memorandum of understanding with a local pediatric clinic chain for all four agencies to ensure families get appointments scheduled in a timely manner in the future. Additionally, the medical school students that complete a rotation through the program have been asked to reinforce the importance of this appointment along with our case managers. While 100% adherence is desirable, we hope that we can make the metric of 75% adherence, up from the 58% just reported within the previous quarter. Feedback will help us make other necessary adjustments, which will help us move closer to our 100% adherence goal at the end of the fiscal year."

Then instead of donors pulling funding, you get them saying, "Great idea, how can we help? Can we purchase bus tickets for the families so they can get to and from their appointments?"

Focus on the data that shows the effectiveness of the organization and your programs instead of (or at least in addition to) data on who is funding you. Align the value proposition behind what you do, rather than how much you need. Know your numbers and be ready to answer questions, both to show how organized your org is and to motivate people to want to help with your mission.

Get started now!

- Your organization needs to know the data on how your actions benefit those individuals who come in for assistance. Find out:

    o What do the individuals served need most? Do you, or how can you, deliver that?

    o What could you achieve with more money?

- What can you achieve with every dollar?

- Quantify these outcomes in every way that you can throughout your organization.

  - If you patch potholes, determine the total cost of each one and build messaging around that.

  - If you offer childcare, calculate the cost per child.

  - At what echelons does that cost reduce?

  - How can you show the effectiveness of every dollar in a way that motives your donors?

- Build systems around collecting all data central to your action points rather than making it an afterthought.

- Look at other charities in your area that have great data game and find out how they do it. Maybe you can partner with them and share resources if they have a data nerd on staff.

- Be transparent with program participants about all data you collect from them.

NO MATTER THE POLITICAL DISCOURSE, DIVERSITY STILL MATTERS (AND NFPS TEND TO SUCK AT IT)

*R*emember when we discussed the importance of demonstrating real impact by being honest about all stats, instead of cherry picking? Here is a :::chef's kiss::: example within a whole new chapter, just for funsies.

Not-for-profit sector research agency Candid published a report in 2024 about diversity in the nonprofit sector. And we can pull statistics from that report that makes the NPO sector seem like a veritable rainbow coalition.

Over half of all nonprofit workers are non-white (53% specifically), which is a better statistic compared to that of the entire U.S. working population. Seventy percent of nonprofit sector jobs are held by women, and 15% by LGBTQ+ individuals (which is two to three times that of the estimated US population of LGBTQ+ folks).

And man, you can feel good about charities when you see numbers like that, right? Except those numbers are about workers, not leaders . . . and the percentages change dramatically once you start looking at positions of power in these organizations.

While NFPs are a female-dominated industry (like elementary school teachers, dental hygienists, childcare workers, etc.), the industry's representation drops once we start looking at positions of power, as noted within the Candid survey. The frustrating truth is this: when it comes to the positions that pay well and allow for decision making? Men tend to rise more quickly into leadership positions, something known as the glass escalator effect.

We see the same effect when we are discussing people of color. The same Candid survey found that two-thirds of board members identified as white, and 70 percent of CEOs were white. BoardSource's "Leading With Intent" 2017 survey found an even more egregious discrepancy. In their survey specifically of nonprofit executives (1,750 of them to be exact), they found that almost 90% of the CEOs and 84% of the board members were white. The Race to Lead survey, published by the Building Movement Project, noted that even for nonprofits who focus on serving people of color, 16% of the boards were all-white.

These variable numbers may be related to the types of organizations that were surveyed. The larger and more wealthy the organization, the less diverse they are. When you parse out the organizations with annual expenses under $50,000, 44% of these organizations are led by executives of color.

Findings from researchers also published in the Race To Lead report found that white-run organizations are far more likely to have larger organizational budgets. They also found that white folks in the sector were far more likely than their peers of color to have another source of household income, were less likely to be supporting family members outside their household, and far more likely to receive additional pay from their NFP employer (in the form of cost of living increases and bonuses).

The same BoardSource survey queried the CEOs in question about whether they, you know, thought that the powerful positions should be less white. Sixty-five percent of them stated that they knew increasing diversity was important, but haven't made it a priority. Forty-one percent of the board members said the same. Only 20% of nonprofit boards reported trying to do something to increase diversity.

Which (back to the Race To Lead report again) makes sense. White respondents reported that their race helped their career, and people of color noted a negative impact on their career advancement. And it's getting worse, not better: the reports of negative impact went up between 2016 and 2019.

How to fix it

The relevance and the effectiveness of any organization is fully dependent on a diversity of voices, including (especially?) those with lived experience around the issues your agency purports to address. Being truly committed to expanding the reach of your organization, and ensuring you have decision-makers on board who are committed to pointing out and rectifying blind spots, will also help your *agency reach.*

You want communities of color to know what you offer? Getting articles printed in ethnic media might be the suggestion of a white board, but a mixed board will know other community leaders, pastors, business owners, and the like and can *give input on messaging* in order to *capacity build* with these *external partners.*

(See what we did there? That's the perfect fancy language for you to use when you are making this same argument).

And this is true of all forms of diversity. An individual who uses a wheelchair for mobility will see things those of us who don't will likely miss. A neurodivergent individual will as well. Queer people will notice things even the loveliest of straight allies may not. Younger people will have a far better sense of how to connect to their peers than us crusty Xers and Boomers. Etcetera etcetera.

Here are a few more reasons why diversity makes your organization stronger:

Let's say you make the decision to ensure your board reflects the community it serves. Not just race, gender, socio-economic status, disability status, etc., but also lived experience. If you are serving people getting sober, you should have people in long-term recovery on your board. And you also have to be willing to hear them. And that may mean making some significant adjustments to how the organization functions before they even come on board.

If this is an existing organization, are there people on the board currently that are less invested in making sure diverse voices are respected and considered? Sometimes the hardest part is not recruiting new folks into these decision-making positions, but knowing if there are other people that . . . no matter how sweet, and kind, and well-meaning even . . . are part of the problem, and not the solution. It may be time to retire some folks.

It's important to turn a critical eye to how the organization will appear to the individuals you want to recruit. One thing Faith and Joe both look at when being asked to participate is: Does the organization cater to donors, or to the people they serve? Once again, that's always the first consideration. If the organization is so fearful of sounding political or leftist or anarchist or challenging in any way, shape, or form? Even if it is just a stance on actively embracing equity in all programming? We know we won't be heard, and so we aren't going to lend our name and support.

Be transparent in these processes. Let the community know you recognize the issue and are actively working to be a more participant-centered program. When someone asks, acknowledge your weaknesses *and what specifically you are doing to improve them.* It doesn't pass muster when someone denies that something is a problem or rejects another point of view outright. Talk like a person sounds, not like a corporate statement of non-responsibility. Be authentic and acknowledge the strong points of the criticism. Also, as mentioned above, in honest data this means owning where the organization isn't doing all it should and could and showing that you are dedicated to getting things right.

And if you are one of the people on one of these boards or you've been invited to join one, and you are not a member of the community that is being served, consider what my friend Pastor Naomi Brown terms "sneaking in the front door." If you get in, you can be the ally that makes all the arguments about more representation and inclusivity. Speak to these needs, and speak loudly. Right people are typically quite unpopular. And yeah, you may be asked to leave (it's happened to both of us . . . much to no reader's surprise). But you also may affect change because you held the door open behind you.

TREAT YOUR STAFF LIKE PARTNERS RATHER THAN PUPPETS

*F*irst of all, we need to clarify that staff doesn't necessarily mean paid employees. You may be operating on a dime and everyone is a volunteer working their ass off for a cause they believe in. We love that for you and for the world in general. So when we say "staff" we are saying "the people providing services and support to the program participants."

And a dysfunctional staff is one of the fastest ways to sink an amazing program. We've already discussed that if your agency is employing folks, they really, really, really need to be paid a livable, fair market wage, and we have the data to back us up. At least if you want to retain employees for more than a year.

The places where Faith has worked the best were the ones that (everyone all together now) *were centered on the participants of the program.* Interviewing included this focus—yes, program participants were on the hiring assessment team for all second interviews. Training included this. Every team meeting, every all-staff, every (data-driven) decision was participant focused. And not in a medicalized, "we're the experts" manner, but in a recovery-focused, "you're the expert on your own life, tell us what recovery would look like for you" manner.

Faith still talks to many of her former coworkers and supervisors from such places, and there is a universal wistfulness for a program culture that is as rare as it is special. And the confusing part is that *it isn't hard to do.*

Divide the work

Remember Amanda Montell on the podcast *Sounds Like A Cult*, cleverly explaining how nonprofits are a cult? So many of her points were that nonprofits exploit their workforce, demanding long hours for low pay because you care. I mean, prove that you care by working harder and longer than we are paying you for. Frankly, this attitude in nonprofits is poor management. Don't become one of those nonprofits. Instead, structure the labor in ways that leverage your goals.

If you are founding or working with others, in order to be efficient, at some point the work will need to be divided. Remember, it's not a valid excuse to be disorganized just because you are a nonprofit. Delegate work based on each person's:

- Individual strengths and skills: Microcosm uses the Clifton Strengths Test, but there are various strengths tests for organizations online. These identify the core of how to apply someone for maximum effectiveness, in addition to the tasks that they naturally excel at.

- Their proclivities: Someone who is very nervous about money will probably do a good job but not have a ton of confidence in the results, so this should be less than a third of their work.

- What they enjoy doing or find meaning in: The values that attracted them in the first place.

You cannot only give someone the work that they want to do or the work that they are good at, but hate. The best practice is really a mix of those three. The work they enjoy is a great reward for the work that they slog through, expect to take hours, and finish in five minutes.

It's counterintuitive, but the best performers are people who aren't entirely confident in knowing what they are doing but are willing to put in the time and effort. They tend to be overlooked by other employers so they work harder to show their abilities.

Over and over, our best hires are the people who don't present confidently but are incredibly competent. Why is this so effective? When someone thinks they *know* something, they put zero forensics into it. They repeat a rote muscle memory towards the task. Results tend to be middling or below. When someone believes that they could have a firmer grasp on something, they research contemporary best practices for how to succeed with maximum effectiveness. They think critically about how to best achieve the desired results. They are well versed in the painful results of failure. They present an informed case about why the task should be handled in the prescribed manner and care deeply about the outcome because they are so invested in it. For any mission-based organization, you are solving a complicated problem that likely persisted across decades or longer. It doesn't have easy fixes, so you need smart people to apply brilliant solutions.

How to do it

Organizational policies work if you enforce them. Everything from attendance to a fair system for raises and promotions—consistently applied—will help your staff to have reasonable expectations and stick around longer. Nobody works at a nonprofit to get the biggest paycheck. But they do feel burned if they don't feel like they are being treated fairly under the circumstances. Similarly, the conscious inculcation of a participant-centered not-for-profit culture will dramatically improve retention. Your staff and your volunteers are the ones providing direct service and support. So the job of everyone else in the organization is to support their ability to provide direct care services.

This means supporting in the present and with an eye to their future in the field. As for *in the present*, we know you are already doing all you can to make sure they are paid fairly, if pay is available. This also means having reasonable expectations of their time. Individuals involved in this kind of work already tend to overwork themselves because they are passionate about the mission. Your job is not to use that against them to do more, but to recognize them and thank them for their dedication—and then make sure they go home. The organization is not their family, and making it out that they should think of it like that is the surest way to invoke burnout.

I am sure your funding sources have metrics that direct-provider staff are meant to achieve. Instead of "coaching" them about the importance of making those metrics—which we all know is just "file documentation designed to paper the worker's eventual dismissal"—and which could lead someone who is already overwhelmed to quit before you fire them or else commit fraud to make your metrics, your job is to find out what they need in order to make the metrics and then do everything humanly possible to get those needs met. It is almost never something expensive and unwieldy to accomplish. One of Faith's favorite examples was finding out that the behavioral health intake team at her agency was doing double data entry, which was why intakes took so long.

(Go figure.)

By diverting funds from purchasing new desktop computers to new laptops, they had the portable equipment needed to only enter data once. Intakes increased by 33% immediately.

(Go figure.)

The other big thing is keeping an eye to the futures of your direct-care workers. There isn't a lot of upward mobility in the nonprofit sector, especially in the smaller organizations that make up the vast majority of the market. Add in the data we discussed in the "DEI-isn't-evil" section, and we see that people of color don't feel the same levels of active mentoring and support in these positions as white folks in the same positions. A manager's job shouldn't just be their employees' goals for the position they're currently in, but in their career in general. And that is one place where we can really show up for the people showing up for us.

Nurturing the futures of your direct-care workers can look like:

1) Asking them what projects they would like to take on, and what skills they want to learn to build their resumes for the future. And then let them cook. This does *not* mean dumping shit onto their workloads because you think it's good for them (and also you totally need it done), but giving them things they are excited to do. Do they want to write a curriculum? Provide inservices? Give them opportunities to do so.

2) Get them into trainings that build their resumes in the same direction. There tends to be lots of grant money out there in support of training nonprofit employees. So much of Faith's clinical training came through these grants at different points in her career. Some were worth as much as

$30K, which she *never* would have paid for herself.

3) Same goes for conferences. Faith has been in places where the same two-person (leadership) team went to every conference. And she's been at other places where they made sure that different staff were able to attend every year. Those staff always came back excited about presentations and resources and training sessions, and that energy went right back into participant support.

4) Consider ways that you can be supportive that are not traditional material supports. Can you give them a flexible schedule because they are a single parent? Create a work-from-home plan for the same reason? Can you cover some of their workload when they are overwhelmed? Can you be proactive regarding toxic workplace bullshit and protect the people who aren't engaging in the toxic elements like gossip

or bullying and either change or remove the forces that are?

5) When they are ready, help them move up, not just on. This can mean writing them superlative letters of recommendation. Encouraging them to go back to school. Using your networks to get them placed somewhere that will be an excellent opportunity for them. Faith has had supervisors that openly said, "This job will be a stop on your journey, and we are grateful for your time and talent . . . but if you are here after you finish school or your internship hours or any other external goal? We're doing something wrong. Go fly." And she has had others who said, "Why are you helping them build out their resume? They will just *leave*!"

People will leave for all kinds of reasons. They may just fucking *need* to. Do you want an ally at a different organization that you can text for assistance on the regular? Or do you want a bitter former employee who tells everyone exactly where and how you were a gatekeeping shitass who they will avoid speaking to ever again? Joe has met many trusted friends because they were being mistreated by a nonprofit. Joe was able to recognize the situation and step in to help.

6) If you think about the long-term career goals of your staff, they will stick around longer and feel positively towards you forever, even if they have to (regrettably) leave. Look at how to simplify their lives through easier workflows. That's something that executives rarely do—consider how a "short-term" "workflow solution" has dramatically negative consequences for the people who have to carry it out. So if you honestly consider this (ideally by doing the work yourself enough to understand the impacts), and simplify or make decisions that acknowledge this, you will build relationships for life.

7) And most importantly, ask your staff for feedback. Ask them what you could do better. Ask them what choices have negatively impacted them, and solicit their ideas for fixing them.

TREAT YOUR DONORS LIKE PARTNERS RATHER THAN DICTATORS

One of the biggest points of contention in the nonprofit world is the role of philanthropists. Most of the arguments in favor of philanthropist funding sound like, "They are filling in the gaps and funding things that are not fundable—things like climate science solutions, DNA sequencing, or disability advocacy— because they are too out of the mainstream to be something a government can spend money on." Of course, if these philanthropists were being properly taxed there would be no gaps, and we would even have funding for interesting and experimental new paradigms without having to appeal to the special interests and egos of where *they* decide the money should go.

Now, there are tons of people out there that fund all sorts of programs simply because they need funding, the system is broken, and they are passionate about the cause. I know people that fund entire organizations and the salaries of the people working there because the work is important to them. They aren't stupid-wealthy and entitled, they are comfortable enough to give back generously, so they quietly do so. One such organization is an animal rescue local to Faith, Kayser Animal Rescue Effort (animalkare.org), that has helped her rescue multiple cats over the years. On a larger scale, other organizations known for that level of generosity are ones we've already mentioned earlier in this book, including GiveDirectly and World Central Kitchen.

How to attract donors

Now, this is going to sound obvious, but most good ideas sound obvious in hindsight.

Attract your donors through performing your services. Make your narrative compelling. You do something for someone. Why are these people in need of your help? Why is this issue important? How can you clearly state your mission to great effect in places where your donors mingle?

Make it easy to donate. It should be possible for someone to follow links to your website on their phone and donate to you while you are sleeping, then receive a nice (automated) message in response.

- Create a system that incentivizes recurring donations. It's easier to give $10 per month than $100 at once.

- Have a plan in place to welcome them with genuine appreciation once they donate. Show them how they are helping through newsletter updates, an emotional social media feed, and special incentives.

- Tap into your donors' values. NPR famously gives out tote bags to their donors that advertise (wait for it) NPR. And in 2025, when the federal government cut $550M in funding, the organization was immediately out in force with an emotional plea for support that brought in record levels of donations from private individuals. Many stations ended up earning *more* money through this pledge drive than they received federally because they used the moment and the messaging to reach the people who cared about them.[18]

- When you have a big success, broadcast it. Show your donors how effective you were with their money, time, and resources.

- There are other, smaller things that you can do, of course. Once you are networked

18 wtop.com/national/2025/09/pbs-npr-stations-working-to-cope-with-and-survive-government-funding-cuts/

into other nonprofit leaders, they can refer evergreen donors who want to support you. Giving money to charity is inherently a selfish act. Donors give money because it feels good to help. Some donors take this to an absurd level and want to compete to see their names in their highest bracketed tiers of donors.

- This brings us to our next point: Create structured tiers to rank your top donors. Who is your biggest donor? Put their name in lights. Show the three below them with slightly less prominence. The five below them will likely aspire to move up the hierarchy. Perhaps there's a group of ten beneath them before you descend into a giant block of small donors.

It's a silly game, but it's motivating for your donors to want to feel competitive with each other.

Always think about what messaging your supporters expect and need to hear from you and why. Sometimes your base needs to know that you're on the case of righting wrongs in the world. Other times your constituents need to hear that you feel their pain, or that you recognize that you made a mistake—and what you are doing to repair their trust. Keep perspective on what the bulk of your fans are feeling and why. It's too easy to fall into a void of trying to please one person at the expense of your entire network.

It's hokey, but consider your role as both echoing the sentiments around you to validate their feelings and moving the conversation in the direction that it needs to go strategically.

Stop throwing parties—at least the ones that cost you money

The issues with large-scale philanthropy are in the operations. There isn't any oversight or accountability if a billionaire wants to fund research into a rare disease that his mom died from, instead of the desperately needed funding for basic diabetes screenings. Or they want to fund a STEM charter school instead of cleaning up the asbestos in a crumbling elementary school in the town they live in. A public official making that decision with proper funding would (hopefully) get his ass handed to him for such a crock of bullshit. But a philanthropist gets lauded for the same choice, enjoying the public attention along with the resulting tax breaks.

Some of the largest philanthropic organizations are entirely opaque about where those funds are going and how much they really are. For example, the Bill and Melinda Gates Foundation health research amounts are available, but the Rockefeller Foundation funds are *so* not (fun fact: the world's first billionaire was Rockefeller).

Again, if these people and corporate entities (also people, according to the US government) were paying their fair share of taxes, we would have a real shot at a well-operating society, *and* they could still easily fund their passion projects.

In the meantime, you are stuck going after funds. We know. So how do you cultivate the kind of philanthropists that will let you run a great program?

First of all, you gotta avoid *The Real Housewives of Bumfuck Gulch* and all that accompanying gala bullshit. You can read a bunch of think pieces on glittery fundraising events and arguments both for and against their ability to raise money for an organization. The quickest response we have to all of them is Roshan Amble's journal article, "An Investigation into the Efficacy of Nonprofit Organizations," in which he combed through all those 990 forms to see if the galas make any money.

Short version: they don't.

And one of the larger arguments about creating an event that produces program solvency is that the event needs to spend big in order to make big, because events don't do well if they are chintzy. Also incorrect, according to Amble's data, which demonstrates that the more you spend . . . the more you spent. With no change in returns.

There are no benefits of significant spending on special events directly, as there is no long-term monetary advantage in doing so. To reach your donors, go small.

Faith has been involved in many agencies that hosted galas that didn't make any money; in fact they seemed to be a great place for people to show off outfits and accessories that cost far more than anything they donated. It is an exhausting and disheartening thing to watch happen, and we can do better. The only ones she's attended that ever raised a damn dime were the DIY-ethic ones, where everything was donated toward the cause so people could show up and have fun . . . even commoners like her and Joe.

Joe worked for one nonprofit whose entire annual operating budget came from a single, scrappy annual event where all of the performers donated their time for the cause. How did we do it?

- Our cost was $0. The venue was donated, the labor was donated, the food was donated, and all of the work was aligning a value chain towards a common goal.

- Nobody personally benefitted.

- Nobody dressed up (Joe wore cutoffs).

- Everyone came together for the benefit of the cause.

At another nonprofit where Joe worked, one employee was exceedingly skilled at rousing morale around creative fundraising strategies, whether that was organizing an art show from a weirdo who lived on the block or creating educational programming for kids.

But that clever employee's greatest victory was that most of the org's funding came from the county, for every pound of trash we creatively kept out of the landfill. We could convince donors to give us things that they were going to throw away, then connect them with organizations, businesses, or patrons who needed them. This could be small donations or large ones, and—

often—if a donor and recipient were working in large enough volume, we wouldn't even need to touch the stuff; we'd get paid just to introduce them. For many years Microcosm received all of our shipping supplies for free from corporations who were throwing them away.

Make donors a part of the team

The Donor Bill of Rights exists and it's a solid document. It was created by the Association of Fundraising Professionals, the Association for Healthcare Philanthropy, the Council for Advancement and Support of Education, and The Giving Institute, who came together to create a bill of rights that states . . . donors, those considering donating, and the general public all want to know how money is being used by these charitable organizations. As well they should.

And we are here to suggest that the best way to do that is to make donors part of the team. Do they get thanks and praise and a plaque for their office and a seal for their website or whatever?

Sure. But the best way to keep them in the loop and invest in their investing is to treat them like a key player, not just a wallet.

Joe sat on the board of one organization where the funders did not provide one iota of feedback to the nonprofit and simply praised the work that we were doing. This was unhelpful. The next nonprofit that Joe was on the board of was unhelpful in the opposite way: The funders provided extensive feedback and attempted to direct the priorities and actions of the organization. This was because the leader was *too* receptive to feedback. If a member made a public stink about anything that they wanted, they were rewarded with a meeting. If a funder complained about a rebranding or a new initiative (usually because the funder was racially tone deaf), the leadership created a feedback-receiving session . . . even though the decisions were already made. This was to smooth feelings, but it wasn't a two-way street.

Often when programs become more inclusive, this tends to rile up people who liked them exclusive. This is true for removing both things like racist figures from history from your programming and roadblocks that truly prevent others from participating.

You don't need to schedule a listening session for feedback that you fundamentally disagree with or won't incorporate. Of course, this is different if you don't yet understand the other person's point of view—which is potentially valuable to ascertain. When you change things, people are going to want to feel like their opinion is heard. This is important up to a point. You simply may disagree with each other. That's fine. And there's little purpose in creating a continuous sounding board.

Otherwise, this is problematic because it means the loudest voices are creating undue influence and redirecting your services away from the people you serve.

Ideally, funders would be close enough to your organization that they understand the organization's decisions, especially if they don't agree or see the whole picture yet. Let funders sit in on board meetings, let them tour facilities, keep them apprised of programming on the regular. Include them in different ways, not just with financial asks. One of the best pieces of advice Faith ever received from a successful nonprofit was to reach out to donors with *all kinds* of program updates. The program director who shared that advice stated his ratio was four general updates about how their investment was yielding return in the program (big wins, new news, etc.) before even one small ask for more money.

I mean yes, your email signature line will have donation links within it, we know. And it should. But it isn't part of the information being relayed. It's just a "we served 30 new families this month, thanks in great part to you believing in our mission" kind of love note. The more involved they are in the inner workings, the more likely they are to see emergent need.

Picture an interested party sitting in on a board meeting where you are looking at a budget shortfall for after-school tutoring or the like. As the board is discussing doing a specific campaign drive to get the needed program up and going, your invested investors may be willing to use their connection to funding sources to get it funded, even if they can't afford to fund it themselves.

Including your donors is also how you inculcate them into the concept that this is a participant-led program. The things the participants identify as their priority needs take precedence over what the rest of us think those needs should be. The stance should always be:

- We listen to the community and provide as much help as we can with the funding we have.

- We don't know people's lives better than they know their own.

- We are providing a community of care that helps them support their best lives.

Faith worked at an agency that defined its recovery focus as the "reawakening of hopes and dreams," and those hopes and dreams were chosen by the program participants, not the staff. Exactly as it should be. Now, the funding source defined a recovery focus around fewer inpatient hospitalization days. And most places would be focusing on medication management, case management, and all those practical support strategies. And we weren't blowing any of that work off. But the priority included helping program participants with their hopes and dreams. This included:

- Helping a client set up a gallery showing for their art. It went fantastically, art sold well, and he went on to establish a career.

- Jamming on various instruments with a client who played guitar during visits. As the client built up their confidence, they started playing in more places and eventually joined a group.

- Another client wanted to get out of the cycle of going to day-hab programs and return to work, and also get a girlfriend. So we prepped for that and he did both. And the girlfriend he got? She was lovely, and he brought her by to meet Faith.

Not everything was a big swing. Sometimes it was to have a pet. Or to be able to go out to lunch at a local restaurant. We did our damndest to make those things happen.

What about the medications and case management needs? Those happened too, because they were now in service of a large goal that brought joy and meaning to people's lives. It's awfully hard to do any of the things above if your symptoms preclude you from doing so, or you don't have a stable living environment to go home to at night.

Was pitching this to funders a challenge? Only until they saw our results.

ALIGN THE VALUE CHAIN

*H*ow many nonprofits have you witnessed having a scandal? Sometimes, the cause for this is that nonprofits set expectations higher. They have declared their set of values of making the world a better place in their eyes. So employees come in bright-eyed, bushy tailed, and idealistic . . . only to find out the dark, inner workings of the organization. Which are often more focused on fundraising than mission.

In most nonprofit work, programs are divided into three areas:

- Service that keeps the beneficiaries happy and coming around

- Things that make money for the organization

- Educational components

In business advocacy nonprofits or other orgs where the beneficiaries are the funders, you'd think that the first and second areas would blend into one—but they usually do not. Often, these organizations are stuck selling services to members that do not provide the stated membership benefits because they significantly fund the organization.

The fact these three areas are distinctly divided is a major hindrance for any nonprofit. Not only because it triples the work and number of departments, but because these departments are categorically at odds with each other. They have different priorities and dependencies.

If there is one lesson from this book, it's to *align the value chain across these three areas as narrowly as possible.* Successful examples of this are shelters that can show their impact through their service, use it to recruit funding, and educate the public about the problem that they are addressing all in their basic service. Nonprofit hospitals receive payment for services rendered and can show the impact of healing the community through this.

Remember the nonprofit where Joe worked who received funding from the government for keeping items out of the landfill through redistributing corporate waste to the public to repurpose? The value chain was aligned because everyone benefited. The nonprofit received funding. The county saved money through these donations because it was cheaper than disposal costs. The public made art and other useful things. The corporations got to feel good about giving away their waste. This allows everyone who touches the process to benefit. And the entire process flowed into fantastic talking points for the public, stories for the evening news, and heartwarming retention for the nonprofit to have repeat visits.

Similarly, educational organizations often receive government funding for providing services cheaper than public institutions can. So the trick, once again, is to streamline your operations to be more efficient—like any other business. That's your value chain. How does your service add value for everyone who touches it? Even donors benefit by giving money because it *feels good* to give money to something that you care about and believe in.

Use the successful utilization of your mission as the primary fundraising tool. Like all good ideas, it seems so obvious in hindsight. But this is the principal strength.

CONCLUSION

A nonprofit is a business. A nonprofit may make money, while a for-profit business may lose money. That's why drawing a distinction between the two can be so misleading.

So what's actually different about a nonprofit? You put the people that you serve first and foremost: ahead of yourselves, ahead of your funders, ahead of your ego, ahead of everything else. When you make any decision, first ask yourself, "What is in the best interest of the people that I serve?"

From there, help them as directly as possible. Can you give them mountains of cash? If not, what's the next best thing that you can give them? If you don't know, *ask them*. Directly. Because, at the end of the day, the more directly you can address a problem head on, the sooner you can make your own role obsolete. Which should be your ultimate goal.

Despite our stories and experiences here, many—but not all—organizations hate staff or board members who are genuinely committed to the cause. The problem is that if board members or staff are too committed to the cause, they start looking under the hood and *noticing things* that could be improved. There are some organizations that love this and others that really just want you to *mind your business*. Look for organizations that want to make real changes and rouse the rabble if that's your thing.

But don't be like one nonprofit who had a party because it claimed to have succeeded at all of its goals when it objectively appeared to have accomplished nothing that year. If your nonprofit does its job well, you will address the needs of the people that you are serving so completely that you don't need to exist any longer. That should always be your ultimate goal: to have nothing left to do, and move on to tackle a new societal problem.

Manage and carry your own data. Know where you are and are not effective. Make changes to become more effective. This allows you to better support the people doing the work by appreciating them more and making their jobs easier and simpler. As you build out these things in tandem, you can show real impact and treat your staff and funders as partners in every success that you have.

Here is a handy review to make sure you're on the right path:

1. Who is your actual client? (The recipient of services? The public? Funders? Members? Your wacko director? Your own ego? Be self-critical)

2. What research have you performed to ensure you are serving your actual client to *their* specifications?

3. How can you help your client as directly as possible, based on talking to them?

4. How can you eliminate general administrative expenses to make your organization as efficient as possible at doing the thing?

5. How can you support your staff in order to be as effective as possible?

6. Have you examined your idealism or done savior behavior or things you might find on the white supremacy culture list?

7. Do you communicate with your donors even when not asking for money? Not just in a general newsletter, but in updates to *them*?

8. How do you demonstrate the real impact of your work?

9. How do you prep your staff for their career advancement and goals?

10. How can you align your value chain?

Remember, this book isn't an indictment of the industry, but a roadmap on how to do it better. There are simply too many trillions of dollars flowing into charities for them not to be more effective. Use the juicy data that we unearthed and make the world a better place! You can be part of reframing the conversation about nonprofits and focus on their primary value proposition, which is allegedly to *help people*, and how to get them back to that focus.

And remember, don't throw fucking parties, they don't make real money. It's just rich person bullshit! If that's your kink, do it on your own time, not on your nonprofit's dime!

GLOSSARY

33% Rule: At least a third of a public charities' annual revenues over a five-year period must be funded by the general public, rather than a few large donors. This shows public interest and goodwill.

501(c)(1): Services of the government, owned and run by the government. You can work for them, but you cannot create one unless you are the government.

501(c)(2): Corporate parent entities that hold title for property owned by tax exempt organizations. Typically this is done to protect the property in the event of liability or a lawsuit.

501(c)(3): The most common type of nonprofit that most people would think of throughout this book. Obtaining this status allows donations to the organization to be a tax writeoff for donors and sufficiently widens the ability to receive grant funding. Food banks, literary associations, churches, schools, and research organizations all fall under this broad umbrella. These organizations are typically thought of to perform services akin to the public good or the government. One notable exception as a result: they cannot work to directly influence elections.

501(c)(4): These are "social good" organizations, like firefighters, Planned Parenthood, or the National Rifle Association. Their donors can be top secret and they can engage in lobbying activities.

501(c)(5): These are labor unions and associations, whose role is to advocate on behalf of their members for better conditions and terms. May engage in lobbying and election influence.

501(c)(6): These are business member organizations for a specific industry. They advocate for better business conditions for that industry, such as real estate brokers or book publishers. Profits cannot benefit a specific person or business. The NFL was once filed as this type of organization.

Accrual Accounting: Financial record-keeping based on when expenses were made rather than when expenses were paid for (which is known as "Cash Accounting").

Advocacy: To advise stakeholders, legislators, or individuals about an issue that affects the membership. Nonprofits may *advocate* on issues that may affect their mission or the well-being of their constituents. Most nonprofits cannot attempt to influence legislation, however.

Annual Report: These summarize both the impacts of efforts as well as showing money received and how it was used. Done well, this is your best marketing tool.

Assets: Property owned by the nonprofit organization. This seems innocuous at first, but in many cases this is where large amounts of money are hidden. A day laborer nonprofit, for example, bought a 2,000 sq. ft. building for half a million dollars to use as an office. You can use the argument that an office benefits their overall organization, but how much work could half a million dollars secure for their constituency?

Board of Directors: Managed by local law in the state of filing, these boards meet several times per year and face term limits so that membership is rotating. They typically contain limits of paid staff that may participate so that the board sufficiently directs the organization rather than the other way around.

Bylaws: You are legally required to have policies for how every aspect of your organization is conducted—from how meetings are run to term limits and selection processes. This is to prevent entrenchment and mismanagement.

Capacity Building: Training your staff so that they can be more effective in achieving your goals.

Fiscal Sponsor: One nonprofit lets another organization use its status as an "umbrella" organization; usually for someone who has not yet obtained their own 501(c)(3) status.

In-Kind Donations: When a benefactor gives you goods or services instead of cash. These are also tax deductible to 501(c)(3) organizations.

Lobbying: Attempting to influence lawmakers to vote a specific way on a specific issue.

Mission Statement: The broad-based goals of the organization in a single sentence.

Pass-Through Funds: Money received by an organization that must be used for a specific beneficiary or given to a specific secondary recipient.

Pledge: Promise to make a gift in the future.

Reserves: The fancy, misdirecting nonprofit term for "profits." It's truly Orwellian. Nonprofits with significant cash reserves often hold investment accounts that accrue in value. But sometimes this is just a bank account with last year's profits. Also sometimes called "Surplus."

Sustainability Plan: Often, when a nonprofit receives a grant it creates sudden momentum on programs. A sustainability plan is your long-term strategy for how to maintain momentum when this funding runs out.

Theory of Change: This is your organization's impact statement; essentially it's your proof of concept. Your theory of change demonstrates how your specific activities are the best method to achieve the goals of the organization.

Vision Statement: Your idealistic, pie-in-the-sky designs for how your organization will reshape the issue that you are focused on across various long-term intervals, usually years.

Working Capital: Money used to pay for operating costs.

REFERENCES

Amble, R. (2023). An Investigation into the Efficacy of Nonprofit Organizations. Open Journal of Business and Management, 11(03), 1130–1157. doi.org/10.4236/ojbm.2023.113064

American Red Cross. (2025, May 20). Charity Navigator - rating for American Red Cross. charitynavigator.org/ein/530196605

Aussenberg, Randy Alison (2018, September 28) "Errors and Fraud in the Supplemental Nutrition Assistance Program (SNAP) sgp.fas.org/crs/misc/R45147.pdf

Baker, D., & Rho, H. J. (2011). The Potential Savings to Social Security from Means Testing. CEPR Reports and Issue Briefs. ideas.repec.org/p/epo/papers/2011-05.html

Bekkers, R., & Wiepking, P. (2010). A Literature Review of Empirical Studies of Philanthropy: Eight Mechanisms That Drive Charitable Giving. Nonprofit and Voluntary Sector Quarterly, 40(5), 924–973. doi. org/10.1177/0899764010380927 (Original work published 2011)

Benjamin, L. M. (2020). Bringing Beneficiaries More Centrally Into Nonprofit Management Education and Research. Nonprofit and Voluntary Sector Quarterly, 50(1), 5-26. doi.org/10.1177/0899764020918662 (Original work published 2021)

Benjamin, L. M. (2012). Nonprofit Organizations and Outcome Measurement: From Tracking Program Activities to Focusing on Frontline Work. American Journal of Evaluation, 33(3), 431-447. doi. org/10.1177/1098214012440496 (Original work published 2012)

Beresford, P. (2023, October 12). Why means testing benefits is not efficient or fair. The Guardian. theguardian. com/social-care-network/2013/jan/14/means-testing-benefits-not-efficient-fair

Bhati, A., & Eikenberry, A. M. (2015). Faces of the needy: the portrayal of destitute children in the fundraising campaigns of NGOs in India. International Journal of Nonprofit and Voluntary Sector Marketing, 21(1), 31–42. doi.org/10.1002/nvsm.1542

BoardSource. (2017). Leading with Intent: 2017 National Index of Nonprofit Board Practices. https://leading-withintent.org/wp-content/uploads/2017/11/LWI-2017.pdf

Bruenig, M. (2020, September 24). The problems with Means-Testing are real. People's Policy Project. Retrieved June 20, 2025, from peoplespolicyproject. org/2020/09/24/the-problems-with-means-testing-are-real

Bruenig, M. (2022, November 11). Universal Benefits Cost Less Than Means-Tested Benefits. People's Policy Project. peoplespolicyproject.org/2022/11/11/universal-benefits-cost-less-than-means-tested-benefits

Bruenig, M. (2022, November 14). Universal benefits are actually cheaper than Means-Tested ones. Jacobin. Retrieved June 20, 2025, from jacobin.com/2022/11/ universal-means-testing-benefits-korpi-palme-taxes

Brumme, C., & Trelstad, B. (2023, May 1). Should your start-up be For-Profit or Nonprofit? Harvard Business Review. hbr.org/2023/05/should-your-start-up-be-for-profit-or-nonprofit

Building Movement Project. (2022). Race to lead Survey key findings. https://buildingmovement.org/wp-content/uploads/2024/01/BMP_RTL_Key-Findings.pdf

Captrust. (2023, May 31). Transparent reputations and nonprofit organizations. CAPTRUST. captrust.com/ resources/transparent-reputations-and-nonprofits

Carnochan, S., Samples, M., Myers, M., & Austin, M. J. (2013). Performance Measurement Challenges in Nonprofit Human Service Organizations. Nonprofit and

Voluntary Sector Quarterly, 43(6), 1014-1032. doi. org/10.1177/0899764013508009 (Original work published 2014)

Charity incentives. (n.d.). plum.xoxoday.com/glossary/charity-incentives.

CommunityForce. (n.d.). Nonprofits are faring poorly with data collection and use communityforce.com/nonprofits-are-faring-poorly-with-data-collection-and-use/

Corbett, H. (2025, February 26). 3 ways business leaders can blend profit with purpose. Forbes. www.forbes.com/sites/hollycorbett/2025/02/26/3-ways-business-leaders-can-blend-profit-with-purpose

Crary, D. Missing-Children Charities are Targeted for Fund-Raising Irregularities. LA Times. latimes.com/archives/la-xpm-2000-dec-31-mn-6753-story.html

DeBenedictis, E. A. (2023, December 7). Erika's quick-start guide to research nonprofits. Erika's Newsletter. erikaaldendeb.substack.com/p/erikas-quick-start-guide-to-research

Daly, M. (2019, April 26). 11 Nonprofit research resources to bookmark now. Whole Whale. wholewhale.com/tips/nonprofit-research-resources

Dodge, J., & Ospina, S. M. (2015). Nonprofits as "Schools of Democracy": A Comparative Case Study of Two Environmental Organizations. Nonprofit and Voluntary Sector Quarterly, 45(3), 478-499. doi. org/10.1177/0899764015584063 (Original work published 2016)

Dunn, A. and Cerda, A. (2022). Anti-corporate sentiment in U.S. is now widespread in both parties. Pew Research Center. pewresearch.org/short-reads/2022/11/17/anti-corporate-sentiment-in-u-s-is-now-widespread-in-both-parties

Charity Navigator. (n.d.). Charity ratings and donor Resources | Charity Navigator. charitynavigator.org

Christiano, A., & Neimand, A. Stop Raising Awareness Already (SSIR). (n.d.). (C) 2005-2025. ssir.org/articles/entry/stop_raising_awareness_already.

Clerkin, C., Diomande, M., Koob, A. (2024). The state of diversity in the US nonprofit sector. Candid. doi. org/10.15868/socialsector.43685

'Daily Show' asks Scott to pee in cup. WPTV News. youtube.com/watch?v=K0TIyuGemAQ

Donor Trust Report | Charity Trust, giving Attitudes, and Trends. (n.d.). https://give.org/docs/default-source/donor-trust-library/2024-give-org-dtr-trust-and-giving-attitudes-across-u-s-regions-and-religious-affiliation-1.pdf

Donorbox: #1 donation software & Nonprofit fund-raising suite. (n.d.). Donorbox. donorbox.org/?utm_ source=GoogleAds&utm_medium=ppc&utm_campaign=Brand&gad_source=1&gclid=Cj0KCQjwqpSwBhClARIsADlZ_TlVVKFpof1COezLD2jKioHN-5c0NCvuj9Ri4qa7toh7xbjsfSOkOossaAkq0EALw_wcB

Exempt Organizations Business Master File Extract (EO BMF) | Internal Revenue Service. (n.d.). irs.gov/charities-non-profits/exempt-organizations-business-master-file-extract-eo-bmf

Exempt organization types | Internal Revenue Service. (n.d.). irs.gov/charities-non-profits/exempt-organization-types#:~:text=Organizations%20organized%20and%20operated%20exclusively%20for%20religious%2C,exempt%20under%20Internal%20Revenue%20Code%20Section%20501(c)(3).&text=These%20include%20social%20welfare%20organizations%2C%20civic%20leagues%2C%20social%*20clubs%2C%20labor%20organizations%20and%20business%20leagues

EveryAction & The NonProfit Hub. (n.d.). THE STATE OF DATA IN THE NONPROFIT SECTOR. In EveryAction and the Nonprofit Hub. cdn2.hubspot.net/hubfs/433841/The_State_of_Data_in_The_Nonprofit_Sector.pdf

Federal Bureau of Investigation. (n.d.). 2020 Internet Crime Report. ic3.gov/Media/PDF/AnnualReport/2020_IC3Report.pdf

Friends NRC. (2024, May 17). Are public awareness campaigns effective? - Friends NRC. friendsnrc.org/friends-resources/building-resources-for-effective-public-awareness-campaigns-a-toolkit-for-practice/are-public-awareness-campaigns-effective/

Gies, L. (2021). Charity Fundraising and the Ethics of Voice: Cancer Survivors' Perspectives on Macmillan Cancer Support's "Brave the Shave" Campaign. Journal of Media Ethics, 36(2), 85–96. doi.org/10.1080/23736992.2021.1898963

GlobalGiving Team. (2021, March 1). How much would it cost to end world hunger? GlobalGiving, Inc. Retrieved June 13, 2025, from globalgiving.org/learn/how-much-would-it-cost-to-end-world-hunger/#:~:text=How%20much%20would%20it%20cost%20to%20end%20hunger%20in%20the,Build%20political%20will.

Greer, L. Z. (2020, January 10). It's my party. Philanthropy 451 by Saving Giving. philanthropy451.substack.com/p/its-my-party

Gugushvili D, Laenen T. Two decades after Korpi and Palme's "paradox of redistribution": What have we learned so far and where do we take it from here? Journal of International and Comparative Social Policy. 2021;37(2):112-127. doi.org/10.1017/ics.2020.24

Hayes, A. (2025, April 10). Means Test: definition, how it works, and examples. Investopedia. investopedia.com/

terms/m/means-test.asp

Herd, P., & Moynihan, D. P. (2019). Administrative burden: policymaking by other means. dx.doi.org/10.7758/9781610448789

Horowitz, S. (2017, December 7). 94 percent of millennials want to use their skills for good. HuffPost. https://huffpost.com/entry/94-of-millennials-want-to_b_5618309

Idealware. (2012). The state of nonprofit data. word.nten.org/wp-content/uploads/2015/05/data_report.pdf.

Independent Sector (2025). Trust in Nonprofits and Philanthropy. independentsector.org/resource/trust-in-civil-society/?gad_source=1&gad_campaignid=2142 2542079&gbraid=0AAAAAolQ-ukGgtO3ahy-IcO0g U5aehfUd&gclid=CjwKCAjwhuHEBhBHEiwAZrvd ctCRHi59A9bGgTGbIqwC7630LIhgk8ng-Pf5UAX-uqvp3tjGTDe6X0xoCf54QAvD_BwE.

Keyrus NORAM- NPO & SLED Team. (n.d.). Top 5 data challenges Nonprofits struggle with the most. keyrus.com/us/en/insights/5-data-challenges-non-profits-struggle-with-the-most.

Kissane, R. J. (2003). What's Need Got to Do with It? Barriers to Use of Nonprofit Social Services. The Journal of Sociology & Social Welfare, 30(2). doi.org/10.15453/0191-5096.2898.

Kordas, K. NFL abandons Tax-Exempt status for some good press and a little privacy | Villanova University. (n.d.). villanova.edu/villanova/law/academics/sportslaw/commentary/mslj_blog/journal_archives/2015/0624.html

Korpi, W., & Palme, J. (1998). The paradox of redistribution and strategies of equality: welfare state institutions, inequality, and poverty in the Western countries. American Sociological Review, 63(5), 661. doi.org/10.2307/2657333.

Jones, M. R., U.S. Census Bureau, Ziliak, J. P., & University of Kentucky. (2019). The Antipoverty Impact of the EITC: New Estimates from Survey and Administrative Tax Records. https://www2.census.gov/ces/wp/2019/CES-WP-19-14R.pdf

LibGuides: Researching Non-Profit Organizations: Home. (n.d.). libguides.lib.rochester.edu/c.php?g=982034.

Lowrey, Annie. (2018). *Give People Money: How a Universal Basic Income Would End Poverty, Revolutionize Work, and Remake the World.* Crown.

Mayall, J. (2024, November 15). Means-Testing Welfare is ALWAYS Dumb. Medium. medium.com/@joemayall/means-testing-welfare-is-always-dumb-0d2779e66716.

McMenamin, L. (March 2020). What Is Mutual Aid, and How Can It Help With Coronavirus? www.vice.com/en/article/what-is-mutual-aid-and-how-can-it-help-with-coronavirus.

McNair, K. (2023, January 2). Here's how much money it takes to be considered middle class in 20 major US cities. CNBC. cnbc.com/2023/01/02/middle-class-income-in-major-us-cities.html.

Mikaelian, V. (2025, March 18). Wealth inequality and power dynamics in philanthropy - Inspiring generosity. strengthening nonprofits. creating impact. Inspiring Generosity. Strengthening Nonprofits. Creating Impact. philanthropy.org/wealth-inequality-and-power-dynamics-in-philanthropy/.

Miao, H. (2021, November 1). Non-Profit Burnout is an Underrated Issue. linkedin.com/pulse/non-profit-burnout-underrated-issue-harrison-miao.

Miller, J. D. (1983). "Scientific Literacy: a Conceptual and Empirical Review." Dedalus. 11: 29–48.

Mittendorf, B., & Hackney, P. (n.d.). Let them eat caviar: When charity galas waste money. The Conversation. theconversation.com/let-them-eat-caviar-when-charity-galas-waste-money-82961.

(Mis)Understanding overhead. (n.d.). National Council of Nonprofits. https://www.councilofnonprofits.org/running-nonprofit/administration-and-financial-management/misunderstanding-overhead

Mitchell, F. (2021, December 9). Nonprofit Leadership Is Out of Step with America's Changing Demographics. Urban Institute. urban.org/urban-wire/nonprofit-leadership-out-step-americas-changing-demographics.

National Center for Charitable Statistics · An Urban Institute website. (n.d.). nccs.urban.org/.

Network Depot. (2024, March 28). Significant positive and negative nonprofit statistics in 2024 - Network Depot. networkdepot.com/significant-positive-and-negative-nonprofit-statistics-in-2024/#:~:text=General%20Nonprofit%20Statistics%20*%20The%20United%20States,representing%20about%206%25%20of%20the%20US%20economy

Next-McGovern Becomes 10th Red Cross CEO in 12 Years. (2008, May 1). The NonProfit Times. Retrieved June 11, 2025, from thenonprofittimes.com/npt_articles/next-mcgovern-becomes-10th-red-cross-ceo-in-12-years/.

Njus, E. Why Portland anarchists are patching potholed streets. Oregon Live. oregonlive.com/commuting/2017/03/why_portland_anarchists_are_pa.html

Northwest Registered Agent (2024, November 11). Why was the NFL a Nonprofit? Northwest Registered Agent. northwestregisteredagent.com/nonprofit/nfl

Nowell, C. (2025, April 12). New Mexico made childcare free. It lifted 120,000 people above the poverty line. *The Guardian.* www.theguardian.com/us-news/2025/apr/11/childcare-new-mexico-poverty#:~:text=As%20pandemic%2Dera%20relief%20funding%20dried%20up%20in,Fund%20to%20early%20childhood%20education%20and%20care.

Nonprofits and Philanthropy. (n.d.). Urban Institute. Retrieved June 13, 2025, from urban.org/research-and-evidence/nonprofits-and-philanthropy.

Nonprofit sector research data. (2024, August 15). Bureau of Labor Statistics. bls.gov/bdm/nonprofits/nonprofits.htm.

Nonprofit Trends and Impacts Study. (n.d.). Urban Institute. Retrieved June 13, 2025, from https://www.urban.org/research/publication/nonprofit-leaders-top-concerns-entering-2025

Okun, Tema. White Supremacy Culture Characteristics. Tema Okun. whitesupremacyculture.info/characteristics.html.

ONDCP. (2013). FLORIDA DRUG CONTROL UPDATE. In FLORIDA DRUG CONTROL UPDATE [Report]. obamawhitehouse.archives.gov/sites/default/files/docs/state_profile-florida.pdf.

Otten, L. (2017, August 3). A great place to work. The Nonprofit Center at La Salle University. lasallenonprofitcenter.org/employee-turnover/.

Palmer, K., CFRE. (2025, April 18). Why Do Nonprofits Struggle with Diversity? Bloomerang. bloomerang.co/blog/why-do-nonprofits-struggle-with-diversity/.

Paynter, B. (2019, January 8). More transparency means nonprofits get more donations. Fast Company. Re-

trieved July 1, 2025, from fastcompany.com/90289331/
more-transparency-means-nonprofits-get-more-dona-
tions.

Peddinti, S. (2022, August 17). 5 Compelling reasons why
Every entrepreneur should consider starting a nonprofit organization. Entrepreneur. entrepreneur.com/
growing-a-business/5-reasons-entrepreneurs-should-
start-a-nonprofit/385599.

Policy Basics: The Earned Income Tax Credit. (2023,
April 28). Center on Budget and Policy Priorities. Retrieved June 20, 2025, from cbpp.org/research/policy-
basics-the-earned-income-tax-credit#:~:text=The%20
Earned%20Income%20Tax%20Credit%20(EITC)%20
is%20a%20federal%20tax,to%20supplement%20the%2-
0federal%20credit.

Price, N. Nonprofits & Diversity: Why a lack of diversity can have a negative impact – BoardEffect. (n.d.).
BoardEffect. boardeffect.com/blog/nonprofits-diversi-
ty-lack-diversity-can-negative-impact-2/.

Ragones, D. (2021, November 29). 76% of nonprofits
lack a data strategy, according to Salesforce.Org report. Salesforce. salesforce.com/news/stories/76-of-
nonprofits-lack-a-data-strategy-according-to-sales-
force-org-report/#:~:text=76%25%20of%20Nonprof-
its%20Lack%20a%20Data%20Strategy%2C,for%20
urgent%20support%20eclipsed%20typical%20non-
profit%20operations.

Research guides: Nonprofit organizations: home. (n.d.). guides.library.columbia.edu/nonprofit.

Results for "What was a Dollar from the Past Worth Today?" (n.d.). measuringworth.com/dollarvaluetoday/relativevalue.php?year_source=1981&amount=100000&year_result=2020

Rosenthal, J. (2024, April 26). This is considered "middle class" income in Washington, DC area. FOX 5 DC. fox-5dc.com/news/to-be-considered-middle-class-in-the-dmv-heres-how-much-money-you-need-to-be-making.

Selden, S. C., & Sowa, J. E. (2015). Voluntary turnover in nonprofit human service organizations: The impact of high performance work practices. Human Services Organizations Management Leadership & Governance, 39(3), 182–207. doi.org/10.1080/23303131.2015.1031416.

Sounds Like A Cult & Magical Overthinkers. (2022, October 4). The cult of nonprofits [Video]. YouTube. youtube.com/watch?v=_CozTl0375s.

Stuber, J., & Schlesinger, M. (2006). Sources of stigma for means-tested government programs. Social science & medicine (1982), 63(4), 933–945. doi.org/10.1016/j.socscimed.2006.01.012.

Suozzo, A., Glassford, A., Ngu, A., & Roberts, B. (2013, May 9). Nonprofit Explorer (home). ProPublica. projects.propublica.org/nonprofits/.

Tax exempt Organization search | Internal Revenue Service. (n.d.). irs.gov/charities-non-profits/tax-exempt-organization-search.

Texas House Bill 82(R) HB 300 - Enrolled version. (n.d.). capitol.state.tx.us/tlodocs/82R/billtext/html/HB00300F.htm

The Donor Bill of Rights. (n.d.). Association for Healthcare Philanthropy (AHP). afpglobal.org/donor-bill-rights.

The nonprofit sector in the US. (n.d.). Indiana Nonprofits Project. nonprofit.indiana.edu/our-focus/nonprofit-sector.html.

The Nonprofit Times. (2019, January 8). Accountants Prove Transparency Boosts Giving. thenonprofittimes.com/accounting/accountants-prove-transparency-boosts-giving/.

The nonprofit workforce shortage crisis. (n.d.). National Council of Nonprofits. councilofnonprofits.org/nonprofit-workforce-shortage-crisis.

Thompson, I. (2024, June 3). Nonprofits less diverse at the top: Candid report shows disparities in leadership - Non Profit News | Nonprofit Quarterly. Non Profit News | Nonprofit Quarterly. nonprofitquarterly.org/nonprofits-less-diverse-at-the-top-candid-report-shows-disparities-in-leadership/.

Thorpe, D. (2018, August 29). How to organize the perfect fundraising Gala. Forbes. forbes.com/sites/devinthorpe/2018/08/29/how-to-organize-the-perfect-fundraising-gala/.

Viergever, R. F., & Hendriks, T. C. (2016). The 10 largest public and philanthropic funders of health research in the world: what they fund and how they distribute their funds. Health research policy and systems, 14, 12. doi.org/10.1186/s12961-015-0074-z.

Vu, V. a. P. B. (2021, May 4). The real reasons many organizations are still unable to diversify their board, staff, fundraising committees, etc. Nonprofit AF. https://www.nonprofitaf.com/the-real-reasons-many-organizations-are-still-unable-to-diversify-their-board-staff-fundraising-committees-etc/

Weldon, M. (2021, December 8). Nonprofits So white: New report on lack of inclusion offers strategies - Race to lead. Race to Lead. racetolead.org/nonprofits-so-white-new-report-on-lack-of-inclusion-offers-strategies/.

Where your career is a force for good. (n.d.). Retrieved June 13, 2025, from americanredcross.wd1.myworkdayjobs.com/en-US/American_Red_Cross_Careers/job/Principal--IT-Disaster-Recovery_RC81485

World Central Kitchen | 7 WCK team members killed in Gaza. (n.d.). World Central Kitchen. https://wck.org/news/gaza-team-update.

Zhou, L. (2021, October 15). The case against means testing. Vox. vox.com/2021/10/15/22722418/means-testing-social-spending-reconciliation-bill.

ABOUT THE AUTHORS

Dr. Faith G. Harper, ACS, ACN, holds postdoctoral certifications in sexology and applied clinical nutrition and is trained in yoga, meditation, breathwork, mindful movement, and all of those other forms of care that make most people avoid her at parties. In the past, she has worked in academia, community mental health, and private practice as a licensed professional counselor. She maintains a connection with academia through her work with the Society of Indian Psychologists. She lives in San Antonio, TX, with her amazing friends and family and terrible rescue cats. She can be reached through her website, faithgharper. com.

Joe Biel is a self-made autistic publisher who draws origins, inspiration, and methods from punk rock to sell millions of books. Biel is the founder and CEO of Microcosm Publishing, Publishers Weekly's #1 fastest-growing publisher of 2022 and #3 in 2023/2024, and WorkingLit, the software responsible for Microcosm's aforementioned success—now available for other publishers. Biel has been featured in *Time Magazine, Publisher's Weekly, Oregonian, Things You Should Know, Spectator (Japan), G33K (Korea), and Maximum Rocknroll,* as well as NPR and PBS. Biel is the author of *A People's Guide to Publishing, Autism Relationships Handbook, Unfuck Your Business, Enduring Legacy of Portland's Black Panthers,* and dozens more. Biel lives in Portland, OR.

MORE BY DR. FAITH

Books

The Autism Partner Handbook (with Joe Biel and Elly Blue)

The Autism Relationships Handbook (with Joe Biel)

Befriend Your Brain

Coping Skills

How to Be Accountable (with Joe Biel)

This Is Your Brain on Depression

Unfuck Your Addiction

Unfuck Your Adulting

Unfuck Your Anger

Unfuck Your Anxiety

Unfuck Your Blow Jobs

Unfuck Your Body

Unfuck Your Boundaries

Unfuck Your Brain

Unfuck Your Break-Up

Unfuck Your Communication

Unfuck Your Cunnilingus

Unfuck Your Friendships

Unfuck Your Grief

Unfuck Your Holidays

Unfuck Your Intimacy

Unfuck Your Kink

Unfuck Your Stress

Unfuck Your Worth

Unfuck Your Writing (with Joe Biel)

Woke Parenting (with Bonnie Scott)

Workbooks

Achieve Your Goals

The Autism Relationships Workbook (with Joe Biel)

How to Be Accountable Workbook (with Joe Biel)

Unfuck Your Anger Workbook

Unfuck Your Anxiety Workbook

Unfuck Your Body Workbook

Unfuck Your Boundaries

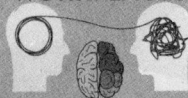

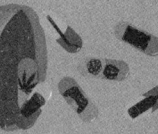